The Full Facts Book of Cold Reading

by
Ian Rowland

———————————————

Publication

The Full Facts Book of Cold Reading
by Ian Rowland

Sixth edition, first revision

Copyright © 2015 Ian Rowland. All right reserved.
ISBN 978-0-9558476-3-9

Previous editions: 1998, 2001, 2002, 2007, 2012.

Published by Ian Rowland Limited

Free Books!

This book comes from:

www.thecoldreadingconnection.com

The Cold Reading Connection is maintained by Ian Rowland. The aim of the CRC is to bring you the best information, training and resources about cold reading and related fields.

The website features lots of information plus a range of books and audio books you can download instantly, FREE of charge!

I am constantly adding to the material on the website, so it's worth checking back from time to time!

- Ian

Dedication

I dedicate this book with love to my Mother and Father, two exceptional, wonderful and admirable people.

I also dedicate it to my partner in life and in love, Careena. Together forever, 'g&s'.

Finally, I'd like to dedicate it with lasting thanks to my many friends around the world who have shared with me their knowledge, respect, love, kindness, fun, laughter, good times, great travel experiences, dreams and miracles of many kinds.

Contents

Section 1: Welcome to the Psychic Circus

*"In the matters of religion, it is very hard to deceive a man,
and very hard to undeceive him."*

- Pierre Bayle. 'Dictionary'

The greatest scam in history?

They are found throughout history.
They are found throughout the world.
And they seem to defy explanation.

They are psychic readings, and everyone has either had one or knows someone who has. People find these readings astonishing, and with good reason, since they are often intriguing and incredible. Let me describe what happens.

You go to see a psychic. She (most are female) has never met you before, yet she describes your personality with pin-point accuracy. She identifies events in your past and present. Her reading may include the names of people you know, and specific facts about your personal life, career, and plans for the future. She seems aware of your innermost thoughts and problems, and she offers glimpses into the future that have an uncanny way of coming true.

This is a psychic reading, and it is the essence of today's psychic industry. Countless thousands have been moved, impressed and thrilled by such readings, offering testimonials like this:

> *"I found my reading absolutely fantastic, I really enjoyed it. Everything that he said was absolutely spot on, and everything that he said that was going to happen to me seems absolutely fantastic. I was very impressed actually. He did a personality analysis on me and it was really right, spot on."*

There are many testimonials like this. If sincere and enthusiastic testimony were an infallible guide to truth, then the authenticity of psychic ability could not be doubted. But it is not. And it can.

The above is a real quote, from a real person. However, the reading she had been given was a complete sham. I know, because I gave the reading and there was nothing psychic about it. Instead, I used 'cold reading' — the psychologically influential technique described in this book.

A global industry, and growing

Glowing testimonials such as the one above are the fuel of today's psychic industry. If people were not impressed by psychic readings, the industry could well collapse. But people are, and the industry is global and growing. Today, it enjoys unprecedented popularity thanks to TV 'infomercials', widespread media coverage and the internet. If you can get online, you can buy every kind of psychic reading under the sun.

As an industry, it may not yet be as big as oil, but it is older, will last longer and is vastly more profitable. To profit from oil you have to find it, transport it, refine it and sell it. To profit from psychic readings, you just talk to people and they give you money. What's more, whereas the world will one day run out of oil, it will never run out of people wanting a psychic reading.

It is hard to say exactly how much talking, and how much money, is involved. In 1998 one source suggested that the psychic network industry in the United States alone would soon be worth 1.4 – 2 *billion* dollars (*see Appendix note 1*). In England, where I live, the industry is similarly flourishing if not quite so well-developed. For one thing, our main TV channels do not accommodate 30 minute 'infomercials'. This is one good reason for living here, and almost makes up for the fact that it rains a lot and nobody looks cheerful.

There are only two ways to account for all these readings and all this money. Either the people giving the readings are genuinely psychic, or they are not. If they are psychic, their clients are paying for access to genuine psychic insight. If they are not, people are falling for a scam. If it is all a scam then it is quite possibly the biggest, most enduring and most popular scam of all time.

The great thing about cold reading, as far as its practitioners are concerned, is that hardly anyone knows about it. In an age when consumers are more cautious and informed than ever before, hardly any of them know the first thing about cold reading.

I cannot prove that psychics use cold reading. However, I can give you all the information you need to decide for yourself.

Welcome to the full facts about cold reading.

What this book is about

The main purpose of this book is to describe how cold reading works in the context of the psychic industry. To this end, the book is divided into six main sections.

You are currently reading **Section One**. This introduces you to the book and to cold reading. Please read this before you read anything else as it will avoid a lot of misunderstandings.

Section Two describes how cold reading actually works.

Section Three features two examples of cold reading taken from my own TV demonstrations.

Section Four deals with Blocking, or making sure cold reading cannot be used on you.

Section Five provides some Additional Notes that conclude the description of cold reading.

Section Six explores Applied Cold Reading (ACR). This is about cold reading techniques used in non-psychic contexts.

The **Appendix** contains supplementary notes and references.

I recommend that you read the sections in order, since later sections build on the information in earlier ones.

What this book is not about

Just by way of helpful clarification, let me mention three things this book is not about. It will save a lot of time.

Are psychic powers real?

This book is not about whether genuine psychics exist. I leave you to decide this for yourself.

There are many people in the world who are absolutely positive that psychic ability exists. Some of them write to me to assure me of this amazing truth, or to tell me that their grandmother was *definitely* psychic or that their dog is. Other people are equally positive that psychic ability is moonshine. Some of these people also write to me, for example to share the latest bit of news about scientific research into paranormal claims. Of course, the 'latest news' in scientific terms has been the same for well over a century now: no psychic powers and no unicorns either.

In one way or another, I have been involved in this debate for over thirty years. I know many sceptics and scientists involved in what is called parapsychology, or the science of studying things that aren't there. Sceptical organisations sometimes invite me to give talks or shows at big conferences, largely because they like seeing me demonstrate a wide range of seemingly psychic phenomena. In my case, having sadly failed to develop any genuine psychic powers, I have to rely on magic tricks, psychology, charm, lying and some not terribly good jokes — but it *looks* the same as the real thing.

I also know quite a few psychics, the majority of whom I find I get along with splendidly.

Personally, I have little time for this long-standing debate between believers and sceptics. It has been going on forever, never goes anywhere and never will. It is inherently sterile, not to say tedious. If you want to know the truth, here it is in eleven words: psychic powers are as real as you want them to be. It's as simple as that.

Are readings beneficial?

Some people defend psychic readings on the basis that people find them helpful or therapeutic. They suggest that whether or not readings are genuinely psychic is unimportant, provided they do some good.

This is an interesting debate, but it has nothing to do with this book. All I am doing in this book is describing how cold reading works in the psychic context. Whether psychic readings are harmful or beneficial is a debate I leave to those who wish to debate it.

Magicians and their methods

This book is not about the methods used by magicians, mind-readers, mentalists and the rest of my kind who practise dark, deceptive arts purely for entertainment purposes.

You may have seen stage magicians who seem able to read the minds of complete strangers in the audience, telling them all sorts of personal details such as when they were born and where they went on holiday. I have done this sort of thing myself more than a few times.

Do these kinds of magic tricks involve psychic ability? No. Stooges and confederates? Not usually, unless the performer is a poor exponent of his craft. So how are they done? Well, you will not find the answers here. After all, if you take away the secrets, you take away the magic, and that's not a fun thing to do.

With very rare exceptions, these stage tricks and mind-reading routines have little or nothing whatsoever to do with cold reading. What magicians do on stage is entertainment. This book is about giving psychic readings, not entertaining people on stage. Please bear this distinction in mind. (Not everyone agrees that this distinction is simple or clear. See Appendix note 2 for more on this point.)

Defining terms

What is cold reading?

Here's a good working definition of cold reading: 'Cold reading is a set of strategies, to do with the psychology of communication, that enable you to influence what others think, feel and believe'.

This book mostly concerns how cold reading is used within the psychic context, by which I mean a situation where someone is giving a reading that is supposedly of a psychic nature. In this context, the cold reading process is used to influence the client's belief that something of a psychic nature is going on.

In the sixth section of this book, I introduce the subject of Applied Cold Reading or ACR for short. ACR is about applying cold reading to non-psychic contexts such as selling, management, negotiation, teaching, therapy and almost any inter-personal situation where influence and persuasion have a part to play. A full explanation of ACR is beyond the scope of this book but is covered in separate material I publish.

What is a psychic reading?

The psychic industry is vast, and accommodates many tastes.

At the junk food end of the market, there are instant phone readings that recycle lame pre-set scripts for every caller. The people doing the talking are trained to say the right things, promise the earth and, most of all, keep the customer on the line for as long as possible in order to turn a decent profit. (There's a perfectly good pun to be made there based on 'prophet' and 'profit', but I'll leave you to make it up yourself.) These conveyor-belt miracles are cheap, quick, and offer mental nutrition on a par with Donald Duck cartoons. This may sound unfair, and it is. I apologise to Donald Duck cartoons.

At the haute cuisine end of the market are one-hour private consultations that cost the earth and deliver heaven on a stick. In the age of the personal trainer and the personal therapist, it should come as no surprise that those with a taste for designer life accessories can hire their very own slice of psy-chic. If presidents and royalty do it, it must be good, right?

To try and cover this rich and wondrous field, I have broken it down into a number of categories.

Readings classified by type

There are many different types of psychic readings. Two of the most popular are:

Tarot. Readings supposedly based on the interpretation of tarot cards and their symbolic meanings.

Astrology. Based on the deliciously absurd creed that studying planets and other heavenly bodies can reveal influences on one's personality or future experience.

In these cases, the person giving the reading may not necessarily claim to be psychic as such. They may claim to have studied what they claim is a valid divinatory science, much as one might study medicine. Other examples in this category would include:

Palmistry. Based on the lines and other aspects of the palm of the hand.

Graphology. Based on a sample of handwriting. (Graphology should not be confused with handwriting analysis, which is a legitimate forensic science used to tell, for example, whether two document were written by the same person.)

Other types of readings are defined in terms of the specific psychic gift claimed by the person giving the reading. Among the more common ones are:

Mediumship. Based on supposed communication with people who have died or, to use the trade jargon, 'passed into spirit'. Also known as 'spiritualism'. Also known as 'exploiting bereaved and vulnerable people for financial gain'.

Clairvoyance. Clairvoyants claim to see or perceive information via psychic sensitivity to some form of energy, vibrations, or impressions. 'Clairaudience' is the equivalent term for those who say their impressions come primarily in auditory form. 'Clairsentience' is the impressively technical-sounding name that covers both of the above, or 'sensing' information.

Psychometry. Touching an object and claiming thereby to sense information about either the owner or events involving that object.

Crystal-ball gazing. Claiming to see or perceive impressions in an orb or similar prop made of crystal glass.

Aura readings. Based on what are said to be coloured human energy fields (wholly fictitious except in the mind of the practitioner) around a person's body.

Intuitive readings. Some psychics prefer to avoid any specific label, and claim only to have a form of loosely-defined intuitive gift that puts them in a position to help people.

This list covers the most popular types of psychic readings, but there are many more besides.

Readings classified by content

The content of readings varies considerably. For present purposes, it will suffice to list three main categories. In order of progressively greater scope, they are:

Health. Readings that focus on health and well-being. Aura readings often fall into this category. Other psychics may choose to specialise in this area, for example reading tarot cards specifically for health indications.

Personality & Character. Concerned not just with health but many other aspects of the client's character, personality and aptitude. For example, this is usually the case with graphology. These readings are sometimes graced with such elegantly pretentious names as 'a psychic character profile' or 'intuitive character analysis'. The nomenclature tends to be shaped by prevailing market trends.

General. Some psychics cover not just health and character, but also seem to perceive specific names, places, dates and events from the client's past, present and future. Clairvoyants usually fall into this category.

Readings categorised by delivery

Psychic readings are delivered in four basic ways.

One-to-one, in person. The most common form of psychic reading is a one-to-one encounter between the psychic and the client. This may take place at the psychic's own den of mystical wonders, the client's own home, or at a psychic fair.

One-to-one, remote. The reading does not have to entail an actual meeting, since psychic services are available by phone, over the airwaves, by post, or via the internet.

Group readings. Psychics sometimes prepare readings for groups. For example, an astrologer may be asked to prepare a horoscope for a group of people deemed to have a common astrological chart (such as all the people in one sports team).

Public readings. Some of the more ambitious psychics give public demonstrations in front of large audiences. This is often the case with spiritualists.

Readings classified by client

As well as there being many different types of psychics and psychic readings, there are different types of clients. The three commonest are:

Personal: Fun. There are people who go to psychics for no particular reason. They may simply be intrigued to see what happens, or regard the whole venture as a bit of fun. Women who work in the same office often organise a group visit to a reader 'for a laugh'.

Personal: Problem. More commonly, people go to see psychics because they are looking for help with regard to a specific issue, concern or problem. This could be anything from advice on romantic or career issues to assistance finding some lost item of great sentimental value.

Corporate. Some companies employ psychics to assist with recruitment and promotion decisions, or other aspects of the company's well-being. This is alarmingly misguided, and could lead to all kinds of prejudice and unfairness.

Now that we have defined 'cold reading' and 'psychic readings', we can define the terms used in the rest of this book.

Terms in this book

In this book I will use the term 'psychic reading' to refer to any or all of the services described above under 'What is a psychic reading?'. The only common factor is the claim, stated or implied, that a person can provide meaningful personal information other than information obtained via:

- the normal human senses (senses regarded as non-controversial by the scientific establishment)

- rational thought

- guesswork and luck

I will use the term 'client' to mean the person to whom the reading is given.

I will use the term 'psychic' to mean anyone providing such a reading and using cold reading to do so. This point cannot be emphasised too much. Let us imagine for a moment that there are genuine psychics and there are people who pretend to be psychic but just use cold reading. *This book is exclusively concerned with the second group.*

Incidentally, this book ought to be welcomed by genuine psychics, if there are any. It will help people to discriminate between authentic psychics, kindly bestowing their gifts upon the world, and shameless fakes.

Popular misconceptions

There are many misconceptions about cold reading. Here are five of the commonest. Each of these may play a part in cold reading, but they are far from the whole story.

Body language

I have often seen people suggest that psychics base their readings on the so-called 'body language' of the client. In case you have been spared exposure to this 'science', body language is a popular term for the study of non-verbal communication, such as stance, facial expression, mannerisms and gestures.

Body language may play a part in cold reading, as we will see later, but it usually plays only a minor role. It plainly cannot help with remote readings (such as readings by phone or via the internet). Moreover, the body language theory cannot account for psychics coming up with names, dates or details about the past.

At the risk of seeming sceptical about everything (which I am not), I might add that in my view body language is a very dubious 'science'. It seems to me that those aspects of body language that hold true tend to be obvious, while those that are not obvious are far from demonstrably true. However, this is not the place for a fuller discussion.

Shrewd observation

Some sceptics suggest that psychics rely on shrewd observation of the client to derive clues about character, career and interests. I feel this notion may owe a great deal to Sir Arthur Conan Doyle's 'Sherlock Holmes' stories. In these justly famous stories, the flamboyant detective often deduces specific details about a person purely by shrewd observation.

This technique is indeed one factor in cold reading. Most cold readers have their own favourite tale of achieving an outstanding 'hit' through shrewd observation. (I have one such story to tell and we will get to it later.) However, this method clearly does not offer a comprehensive mechanism for psychic readings. Some psychics give readings to clients over the radio, by phone, or via the internet. Others frequently produce information that could not feasibly be attributed to such clues. Plainly, there is more to the psychic arts than smart observation.

I would like to add that the potential for deducing information in this way in real life is far more limited than fictional tales and some sceptical literature may suggest. However, even accepting that deductive observation can sometimes work very well, this is in some ways an irrelevance. Cold reading is not primarily concerned with providing accurate information, howsoever obtained. It is about seeming to provide information when in fact there is little or none to offer.

Fishing

Another popular theory holds that cold reading is all about 'fishing' for clues, which is to say trying to elucidate information from the client without this being obvious. There is an element of truth to this. Cold reading *can* involve subtle ruses to obtain information (as well as some that are as subtle as a dropped piano).

However, 'fishing' is simply one small part of the complete explanation. What is more, it is simply too bald a description for what is actually involved. The art lies in the details of how the fishing is accomplished, and how the information obtained is then used in the context of the reading.

Vagueness

Some people suggest psychic readings consist solely of vague and generalised statements that could mean almost anything. I am surprised how often this misleading theory is offered by people who should know better, including supposedly well-informed sceptics.

The 'vagueness' theory only holds good for the most trite and superficial aspects of the psychic industry. A perfect (and perfectly inane) example would be the horoscopes printed by newspapers that (a) cannot find anything better to print and (b) are content to treat their readers as superstitious idiots.

In all other cases, this theory does not hold water. Many cold readers give their clients very specific information, such as names, dates and detailed descriptions of people and places.

Later on this book, you will hear about a psychic who told a client the *exact* name of her brother without guesswork, clues or prior information. In another case, a psychic accurately described the rather unusual job a client did *26 years previously*. In both cases, I was the 'psychic' involved. How was I able to produce such amazingly specific information? All will be revealed later.

Gullibility

Some suggest that anyone who consults a psychic, or believes in psychic readings, must be gullible, credulous or just plain stupid. This is quite plainly at odds with the facts. There are countless clients who, by any criteria, are highly intelligent and perceptive people.

If you have a good grasp of how cold reading works, and how to block it, then it cannot be used on you. Otherwise, it can. It makes no difference how smart, highly-qualified or intellectually brilliant you may be. These qualities do not present any difficulty to a good cold reader.

Incidentally, the same is true of any kind of skilled deception. If you know how the deception works, then you cannot be deceived by it. If you do not know, then you can. A rocket-scientist can be fooled by a deceiver, because she knows about rocket science and not deception. Expertise in one field does not automatically transfer to another.

What is more, deception itself is an extremely vast and complex field. It can easily occupy a lifetime of study, and embraces many specialised arenas. Experts in one area (such as card sleights or gambling scams) may know next to nothing about other areas (such as metal-bending and cold reading).

Section 2: How Cold Reading Works

*"The power of accurate observation is often called cynicism
by those who have not got it."*

- George Bernard Shaw

Notes about the explanation

Seven subsections

The explanation is divided into seven sub-sections. They are:

1. The Set Up. Techniques used by the psychic to get the session off to a good start.

2. The Main Themes. The themes that provide the framework for the reading.

3. The Main Elements. The different kinds of statements and questions that make up the reading. 38 different elements are described, divided into 4 groups.

4. The Win–Win Game. How the psychic can turn a 'miss' into a 'hit', and otherwise recover from errors.

5. Presentation. Aspects of presentation that can enhance the reading's effectiveness.

6. Putting It All Together. How the psychic weaves all the above into a successful reading.

7. Handling Sceptics. How the psychic handles sceptical or 'difficult' clients.

Default example: one-on-one tarot

It would be impractical to relate *every* cold reading technique to *every* type of psychic consultation. I have therefore used a one-on-one tarot reading as my default example. The same principles and techniques can be adapted to deliver all the other types of readings listed earlier.

About the fictitious dialogues

Section Two features numerous dialogues between psychic and client. These dialogues are purely hypothetical, and intended to illustrate *typical* psychic readings. They are based chiefly on my own experience, plus information from other performers and researchers.

In contrast, section Three of this book, 'Demonstrations', contains genuine transcripts of actual readings I have given under test conditions for television. Please bear this distinction in mind.

About the female pronoun

Throughout this section I have used the female pronoun when referring to the psychic and the client. Male psychics and clients do exist, but they are very much in the minority. It therefore seemed appropriate to use 'she' in most instances.

Why are most clients women?

It is interesting to speculate why the great majority of clients are female. It has nothing to do with gullibility, and anyone spouting such views should be tied up in a sack and jumped up and down on until they promise to talk sense.

I think there are two possible reasons. The first is that many social and cultural factors encourage women to credit themselves with 'intuitive' gifts. This in turn may make them more receptive to the notion of someone being able to know things that are, by normal means, unknowable.

Secondly, social and cultural factors also encourage men to cultivate an image of strength and independence. Seeking outside advice runs contrary to this image. Women are less prone to this type of insecurity, and are generally readier to consult others for guidance.

How CR Works 1/7: The Set Up

Before the reading itself begins, the cold reader can take some preliminary steps to get the reading off to a good start. The basic idea is to encourage a relaxed and co-operative atmosphere so that the client will neither challenge nor impede the cold reading process. Here are some common techniques for achieving this goal. Some psychics may use all of them, while others may only use one or two.

Meeting and greeting

Although some psychics specialise in 'mail order' or remote readings, most are in the business of meeting and greeting people. If the psychic is a naturally likeable person, meeting people isn't a problem. Other psychics, less gifted with natural charisma, may employ a range of techniques to help first encounters go well.

There are many such techniques, and they tend to feature in books written for sales people and business negotiators. One good source is Nicholas Boothman's 'How To Make Anyone Like You in 90 Seconds Or Less' (*see Appendix note 3*).

A comprehensive treatment of this subject is beyond the scope of this book. However, I would like to mention what I believe to be the single most effective technique of all: mind scripts.

Mind Scripts

A mind script is a short, simple description of how you want or intend the meeting to go. A good formula for a mind script is three short positive statements like this:

"I like you, you like me, this will go really well."

Using a mind script is *very easy*. You *mentally* recite it to yourself as you prepare to meet someone, and then occasionally re-run the script in your mind during the meeting. At the risk of stating the obvious, you do *not* say it out loud.

You might think that using a mind script during a conversation would create some mental confusion or distract you from what is being said. If you try it, you will find this is rarely if *ever* a problem. So long as you keep the mind script short and simple, you can run it through you mind every once in a while without any problems.

Mind Scripts are a simple way to modify several aspects of the way you communicate. How you come across to people depends on many things, not just what you say. Your body language, tone of voice, facial expression, gestures and energy levels all play a part. If you consciously try to modify all these aspects of communication at once, you will find it more or less impossible. However, running a mind script takes care of all these other things for you. The script acts like a kind of 'master control' that modifies your stance, tone of voice, gestures and so on.

Encouraging co-operation

The psychic takes care to mention that the tarot is not an exact science and involves some aspects of *interpretation*. The point is to plant the idea that she and the client are supposed to *co-operate*. For example, the psychic might say:

> "I won't necessarily always know exactly what the cards are trying to say. Sometimes it's unclear, like looking through a mist, and the exact meaning will actually be clearer to you than it is to me! So bear that in mind, won't you?"

This encourages the client to actively participate in the reading, rather than being a passive recipient of the psychic's wisdom.

The real point, plainly enough, is to encourage the client to provide information and help the psychic to get things right. Many clients require little persuasion to do this. If the psychic offers a statement that is simply wrong, some clients actually *apologise* for not being able to see how it fits!

Most clients want the reading to go well and are therefore keen to help in any way they can. After all, a reading that does not go well is essentially a waste of time and money.

Many clients reveal what is on their mind and *what they want to hear* at more or less the first opportunity. This does rather take the skill and challenge out of the process, and diminishes the relevance of the adjective 'psychic'. However, few psychics complain if this happens.

Intimate atmosphere

The psychic tries to establish a fairly intimate atmosphere for the reading. The specifics are largely a matter of personal style. She may use a slightly softer voice than normal, or adopt a very sympathetic and non-confrontational stance to foster rapport.

Decoration and 'ambience' may also play a part. Some psychics give readings in a room specifically decorated for the purpose, featuring framed prints of a suitably mystical nature, soft lighting, incense, relaxing 'ambient' music and so on. In effect, they are turning the reading into a theatrical performance and setting the stage accordingly.

It would be wrong to suggest that all psychics go down this route. Some prefer to cultivate the clean-cut image of a professional business consultancy. To this end, they may use appropriate furnishings (such as big leather sofas that threaten to swallow you completely) and the props you find in a typical small office (out-of-date year planner, broken computer and a jammed photocopier).

No matter how this intimate atmosphere is created, the point is to dissuade the client from being too challenging or assertive. It also promotes the sense of participation in a *ritual*.

Rituals are a time-honoured way of constraining normal mental responses (including the 'Wait a minute, this is all nonsense' response) and thereby conditioning behaviour. This is why rituals feature in every religion and military organisation. The more time we invest in a ritual, the harder it becomes to break free of it.

Credentials

The psychic conveys the idea that she is well-accredited, experienced and confident. There are many ways of doing this either tacitly or explicitly.

One of the commonest is to display testimonials from previous clients. Another is to display certificates from some palace of erudition such as the 'Something-somewhere Centre for Tarot Studies'. These testimonials and certificates may be genuine. Then again, in this day of cheap computer publishing and 'instant print' shops, anyone can create and frame their own.

Another neat ruse is to have a couple of appropriate reference books on hand, encouraging the idea that the tarot (or whatever the chosen discipline happens to be) is a vast field of study. It is a cute theatrical touch, in the course of a reading, to reach for some weighty reference tome in order to 'clarify' a fine point of interpretation!

Another way to boost credentials is to use good quality props. Tarot cards that are well-made and beautiful carry more conviction than ones resembling free prizes from a cereal packet.

I use 'The Medieval Scapini Tarot' deck produced by U.S. Games Systems Inc., Stamford, Connecticut.

I have no links with U.S. Games Systems and this is an unbiased endorsement. However, if U.S. Games Systems were to offer me free decks of cards (or large bundles of money) as a goodwill gesture, I would be happy to accept them without compromising my integrity in any way. They might like to consider that in future editions of this book my endorsements may have veered towards *other* card companies who are perhaps a little more appreciative of my judgements.

It can help to use cards that both look and feel as if they are very old. One way is to go to a card collector and buy cards that really were made a long time ago. The other is to get a new deck and artificially age the cards. Even the amateur forger's all-purpose ageing formula — a dip in cold weak tea plus gentle baking in the oven (the cards, not the forger) — can produce good results.

What the psychic actually says is also obviously a factor. She may hint at some of the VIPs who use her services, and make veiled references to moving in exalted celebrity circles.

Celebrity endorsements carry a lot of weight in the psychic industry as they do almost everywhere else. Of course, they make little sense. The ability to earn a living as an actor or TV presenter does not make one especially well-qualified to assess psychic ability. However, we live in a celebrity-worshipping age where almost any association with fame or media stardom is good for business. The psychics of the world have not been slow to appreciate this point.

Belief system

As well as establishing her own credentials, as above, the psychic also establishes the credentials of the tarot or whichever divinatory system is on offer. This leads the client to take the proceedings seriously, if not necessarily solemnly. For example, the psychic may refer to the tarot's long history (which is indeed impressive and interesting) or to the many clients who have benefited from its insights.

Such remarks condition the client to respect the psychic proceedings, rather than realise how ludicrous they are. They steer the client to view the reading as a significant revelatory process involving a precious source of wisdom. In fact, the client is simply handing over money to have someone talk to her.

This initial bolstering of the belief system also discourages awkward questions. It does not help proceedings if the client asks how 72 bits of pasteboard, bearing pretty pictures derived from medieval European sources, can yield information about one's romantic options and career prospects.

This aspect of the set up is continued during the reading itself, as we will see later. In passing, I should mention that this kind of ploy seems especially common among astrologers. Some of them drone on about everything from ancient Babylonians to famous politicians in such a way as to make one's ears bleed. However, most are smart enough to realise that boring the client to sleep within the first five minutes, while certainly no impediment to success in the psychic industry, is not generally considered the best approach.

Excusing failure

In her introductory remarks, the psychic usually offers an up-front excuse for any outright failures that may arise later. She also makes it clear that she does not claim to get everything right all the time. For example, she might say something like:

> "I'll be honest enough to admit to you now that I do sometimes make mistakes. It would be wonderful to be absolutely spot on all the time, but after all, I'm only human, and I can only do my best for you. Do you understand?"

This appears endearingly honest, and guides the client to view the psychic's efforts sympathetically. It also prepares the client to help as much as possible (most clients do not take any pleasure in seeing the psychic struggle).

Said in a cheerful and appeasing way, such remarks can get readings off to a flying start. The real purpose, of course, is to make it easier for the psychic to retreat from any completely wrong statements that she makes in the course of the reading.

Recent readings

The psychic asks if the client has had a reading before, and if so how long ago. The main reason for doing this is to avoid inadvertently giving conflicting readings to the same person! Provided two or three months have passed, any discrepancies between the last reading and the current one can be attributed to changes in emphasis, interpretation or 'influence'.

The psychic may also take the trouble to mention that she uses a very unconventional system, or one that she herself has evolved over many years. This helps to cover up any discrepancies between what she says and what other psychics may have said.

Setting the client at ease

The psychic tries to be as welcoming, charming and innocuous as possible. She strives to establish a convivial and friendly rapport, and to get on friendly first-name terms if this is at all appropriate.

This may sound like nothing more than common courtesy, but the point is to overcome any natural reserve and defensiveness the client may have. Some psychics, especially mediums, like to offer endearing introductory statements along these lines:

"May I welcome you in a spirit of love, and say how happy I am to share with you the gifts that come to us all from a higher source."

The psychic also watches out for any fear or anxiety that could obstruct rapport. For example, some clients are wary that the psychic will discover too much or see bad news. It is a good idea for the psychic to eliminate such apprehension, like this:

"Let me say right from the start that there's nothing to worry about. We're here to look at the positive trends in your life, and it's really all about helping you to make the most of what lies ahead. There may be a lot more good news than you realise! Of course, there's a mix of light and shade in everyone's life, but I like to concentrate on the sunshine rather than the rain, do you see what I mean?"

Progress Review

This concludes The Set Up. This is the first of seven sub-sections into which Section Two is divided. Next, the Main Themes that arise in psychic readings.

How CR Works 2/7: Main Themes

So far we have looked at how the psychic tries to set up the reading in a way that is likely to produce a successful outcome (getting paid). The next stage is to actually start the reading itself.

Psychic readings consist of *themes* (what the psychic talks about) and *elements* (what she actually says). We will look the elements in the next section. Themes provide the underlying shape and structure for a reading and ensure it is relevant to the client's life. Cold readers rely on four chief themes:

Love, romance and relationships

Money and material comforts

Career and progression

Health and well-being

There are also three minor themes. These are generally not as important as the main four, but they can prove very fruitful:

Travel

Education and the pursuit of new knowledge

Ambitions, hopes and dreams

It is important to note that all these themes lend themselves to very broad interpretation. 'Travel' can be interpreted literally ('A journey across water') or figuratively ('A voyage from loner to lover'). 'Education' may refer literally to time spent in school or college, or it may refer to lessons learned from life.

Experience suggests these are the themes that most clients are most likely to be interested in, most of the time. Now we can look at the actual elements of the reading.

How CR Works 3/7: Main Elements

So far we have looked at The Set Up, and the Main Themes around which the reading is built. But what does the psychic actually say?

For very simple readings, the psychic may rely on what is more or less a set text, or a set of prepared and memorised scripts. These are known as 'stock' readings. I have included a section on stock readings in Section 5, 'Additional Notes'.

The 'stock' approach to psychic readings, while it can suffice in some circumstances, is simplistic, seldom very convincing and does not constitute cold reading in the true sense.

Cold reading in its most versatile form does not involve a rehearsed script. Instead, it involves numerous different *types* of statements (and questions) that can *appear* more significant or meaningful than they really are. I am going to call each of these an 'element'. The cumulative effect of these elements is to create the illusion that a reading of a psychic nature is taking place.

I am going to describe the 38 most useful and productive elements I know. I have given them pet names for ease of reference, and divided them into four groups:

- about character
- about facts and events
- about extracting information
- about predicting the future

These are not meant to be hard and fast divisions. Some elements listed in one group could just as easily have been listed in another.

In reading about these elements, you may like to bear in mind that later sections deal with:

- what the psychic does if the elements do not work ('The Win–Win Game')
- how *presentational* factors play their part ('Presentation')
- how the whole cold reading process comes together ('Putting It All Together')

Elements about character

This first group of elements are chiefly concerned with the client's personality and character.

Rainbow Ruse

The Rainbow Ruse is a statement that credits the client with both a personality trait *and* its opposite. Here is an example:

> "You can be a very considerate person, very quick to provide for others, but there are times, if you are honest, when you recognise a selfish streak in yourself."

In this example, the client is being told that she is both *selfless* and *selfish*. There are countless variations along these lines: being both introvert and extrovert, shy and confident, responsible and irresponsible. It covers all the possibilities from one extreme to the other, just as a rainbow encompasses all the colours.

The Rainbow Ruse is a very common element in cold readings. It sounds good and seems perceptive. Here is another example:

> "I would say that on the whole you can be rather a quiet, self-effacing type, but when the circumstances are right, you can be quite the life and soul of the party if the mood strikes you."

These kinds of statements are not hard to make up. First, think of a common personality trait. Then describes the client as both having this quality and lacking it. Finally, join the two halves together by referring to time, context, mood or potential. The example given above uses the link, 'when the circumstances are right'. Other good links are 'at other times...' and 'yet you have the potential to be...'.

As well as being simple and effective, this element also affords plenty of scope for some gentle humour based on typical human failings. Here is an example:

> "There is an inherent capacity here for neatness, which is to your credit, but I sense that this capacity does not always prevail, and you can, in some circumstances appear a little deserted by this instinct!"

Rainbow Ruse statements work because most personality traits are neither static nor quantifiable. Very few people are outgoing *all* the time, or introverted *all* the time. Most of us manifest both tendencies from time to time. What is more, there is no objective way to assess where one lies on the graduated scale between extremes of introverted or outgoing behaviour.

Avoiding the quantifiable

The lack of any quantifiable refutation is an important aspect of the Rainbow Ruse. These types of statement do not really work when dealing with quantifiable characteristics.

To see what I mean, imagine that an inexperienced cold reader decides to touch on career issues. She might decide to comment on the client's facility with computers and new technology:

> "There are indications here that you are in tune with the modern world, and that new technologies such as computers and the internet hold few fears for you. However, at times you have found this area quite daunting. Like many people, the era of the microchip has occasionally left you baffled."

This is a perfect Rainbow Ruse in terms of *structure*, but it is flawed. The trait under discussion is quantifiable, and hence susceptible to factual refutation. The client might reply:

> *"Actually, I've been running a data processing department for fifteen years, and I also lecture on emerging technologies. I've never found it daunting in the slightest."*

This error isn't a problem for the psychic as there are many ways to handle it (see later, 'The Win–Win Game'). However, this example shows why the Rainbow Ruse is usually applied to less quantifiable characteristics. It also illustrates the need to couch psychic readings in terms of potential rather than actuality.

Fine Flattery

Fine Flattery statements are designed to flatter the client in a subtle way likely to win agreement. The usual formula involves comparing the client to 'people in general' or 'those around you', and saying she is a slight but significant improvement. Consider this bad example:

> "You are very honest!"

This is certainly flattering, and it may even be true, but it is a very poor piece of cold reading. The first problem is that it sounds like pure flattery, because that's all it is. Most people are suspicious of this kind of blatant flattery and reject it out of hand. Secondly, it lacks any relevance to the psychic system that is theoretically being used. Thirdly, it omits the reference to other people.

The same statement can easily be turned into a successful piece of Fine Flattery. Suppose the psychic has been given a watch that belongs to someone, and is giving a psychometric reading (a character reading supposedly based on an article owned or used by the client). It might go something like this:

> "I sense that the owner of this article is a little bit more honest and conscientious than many people. Not a saint, not perfect, but let's just say that when it really matters, this is someone who understands the importance of being trustworthy. This person has sound values that they try to live up to, even if they perhaps don't always succeed."

This entire spiel amounts to 'you are basically honest'. However, it *sounds* like a perceptive statement.

Honesty is a good basis for a Fine Flattery element, since the vast majority of people are inclined to think of themselves as honest. Several other personality traits can be used in the same way. Among the more reliable are:

- being hard-working and diligent

- fair-minded

- warm and loving

- independent

I must mention to two characteristics that are Fine Flattery gold dust. They always work, always impress, and can carry a thin reading a long way. I have learned to keep them in reserve at all times, like emergency parachutes. Here they are:

- being wise in the ways of the world, a wisdom gained through hard experience rather than 'book learning'

- knowing how to be a good friend

Just for the sake of another example, here is how a spirit medium might apply the same element. Suppose that the medium is supposedly receiving messages from a deceased relative and the Fine Flattery is based on 'You are wise'. It might sound like this:

> "I have your late sister with me now. She says she always admired you, even if she didn't always show it. She says you are in many ways more shrewd than people think. She always thought of you as quite wise, not necessarily to do with books and exams. She means wise in the ways of the world. She's laughing because she says it's wisdom you have had to learn the hard way!"

A cute touch is to flatter the client in ways that ease the cold reading process itself. For example, if the psychic flatters the client as being very 'open-minded', the client is more likely to accept the reality of psychic ability in general.

Psychic Credit

Psychic Credits are character statements that credit the client with some form of psychic or intuitive gift, or at the very least a receptivity to others who possess such gifts. This may be seen as a very specific application of Fine Flattery.

As with the Fine Flattery element, it is not good enough to simply praise the client and hope she likes it. This would be rather clumsy and could make the client suspicious. A more subtle approach is required. Here is how it might sound in a tarot reading:

> "This card, the King of Wands, often indicates a perceptive or psychic ability of some kind. Of course we all have these gifts, but they vary from person to person. In your case, it's the second card in the higher triad, which is devoted to your personal profile. This suggests you have a vivid intuitive gifts. Since you also have the Eight of Coins in support of the same line, I would say you have a kind of psychic talent when it comes to financial affairs. You can perceive value in ways that not everyone else can."

Just in case some clarification is required here, this example also incorporates an element called the 'Jargon Blitz' that we will look at later. Phrases like 'higher triad' and 'in support of the same line' are just made-up nonsense. However, they *sound* good, which is all that really matters.

The Psychic Credit crops up in many different readings. Rare indeed is the psychic who would inform a client that she *lacks* this kind of faculty. The Psychic Credit is often accompanied by little 'proofs' that sound like this:

> "There is an indication that you yourself have quite a well-developed psychic sense. You're probably the type of person who thinks about someone you haven't heard from in a while, and then out of the blue they phone you at that very moment!"

Many clients readily confirm that this kind of thing has happened to them, and it may well have done. As sceptics never tire of telling us, such incidents are far from evidence of psychic intuition. You probably think about people you know fairly often, and you probably receive many phone calls. As there's usually no correlation you don't think twice about it. When, by chance, the person you have been thinking about *does* happen to call, it seems remarkable and you remember the incident.

Male and female psychic credits

There are many anecdotal snippets used to lure clients into crediting themselves with psychic sensitivity. Here is a fairly common one that is offered to female clients:

> "You probably have innate psychic sensitivity that plays little tricks on you all the time. The sort of thing where you feel you ought to smarten up your make-up for no reason, and then suddenly there's a knock on the door and it turns out to be someone you're really glad you looked your best for."

For male clients, the Psychic Credit may be expressed in a form more likely to appeal to the male ego:

> "Even though you are highly pragmatic, you do have some psychic acumen. You're very shrewd, and you can read people very well, like a sort of sixth-sense, making you a good businessman or negotiator. Your intuitive side gives you a lot more rapport with women than most men, and this is something a lot of women find very appealing about you whether you realise it or not."

The Psychic Credit is a very dependable cold reading element, and has the obvious additional benefit of bolstering the belief system that supports psychic readings (which we saw is part of The Set Up, 'Establishing the belief system').

Sugar Lumps

Sugar Lump statements offer the client a pleasant emotional reward in return for believing in the junk on offer. In general, the Sugar Lump relates to the client's willingness to embrace the psychic 'discipline' involved in the reading, and to benefit from the insights thereby gloriously revealed:

> "Your heart is good, and you relate to people in a very warm and loving way. The tarot often relates more to feelings and intuition than to cold facts, and your own very strong intuitive sense could be one reason why the tarot seems to work especially well for you. The impressions I get are much stronger with you than with many of my clients."

It is more or less mandatory to praise the client for being 'open-minded' and 'receptive to many different kinds of wisdom'. This is as sly as it is insidious, since the more the client is disposed to believe in the nonsense on offer, the easier it is to (a) take her money, (b) send her away happy and (c) keep her coming back for more (preferably with a large group of friends).

Sugar Lumps can also be used to weaken resistance to psychic nonsense, or to soften rather inconveniently sceptical attitudes. In these cases, the Sugar Lump is modified to point out what a nice, loveable person the client *could* be, if only she would be less sceptical:

> "I feel in some ways that you have become very defensive, like you're locked up in your own secure little castle. This is a shame, because to some extent you're pushing away a lot of light and love that could be yours. There are indications of a need to take a broader look at life, and to be more open to new ideas even if they may seem a little strange at first. Who knows, you might find a few of the answers you've been looking for!"

This is no more than an emotional punch in the face (albeit very sweetly delivered), exploiting the natural human desire to be accepted and loved. The Sugar Lump may also stress how negative it is to doubt, question or disbelieve. In addition, the psychic may be inclined to throw in a little science-trashing just for added effect. It is all good for trade.

Jacques Statement

This element consists of a character statement based on the different phases of life that we all pass through. It is named after Jacques in Shakespeare's 'As You Like It', who gives the famous 'Seven ages of man' speech.

Jacques Statements are derived from common rites of passage and typical problems that we all encounter on the road to mature adulthood. In this context, many cold reading sources refer to Gail Sheehy's book 'Passages' (*see Appendix note 4*). This remarkable book analyses what Sheehy has dubbed 'the predictable crises of adult life', and remains an invaluable source for anyone wishing to study this territory for cold reading or any other purpose. My own copy is very well-thumbed.

Here is an example of a Jacques Statement, taken from my own readings. It is most appropriate for someone in their mid- to late thirties or early forties:

> "If you are honest about it, you often get to wondering what happened to all those dreams you had when you were younger and all those wonderful ambitions you once held dear. I suspect that deep down, there is a part of you that sometimes wants to just scrap everything, get out of the rut, and start again but this time do things *your* way."

Like many of the elements listed here, the Jacques Statement may seem rather lame on the printed page. However, in the context of a supposedly psychic reading, with the correct presentation and delivery, it can be highly effective.

The Frustrated Talent

Here is another Jacques Statement. This would be suitable for a younger adult, say in her early twenties, who is still developing her career:

> "If you are honest about it, you often feel a sense of frustration that your own ideas, talents and abilities aren't always fully recognised. There have been occasions when you had to fight for the chance to show people what you can do. While you are mature enough to recognise that you have plenty to learn, you often find other people too set in their ways to appreciate the contribution you could make if only they would let you."

This element is applicable to many kinds of readings. I know from experience that it sits very well in a tarot or astrological reading. I am the first to admit that many of the elements listed here can go wrong (hence the later section on getting out of trouble, 'The Win–Win Game'). However, a well-delivered Jacques Statement rarely meets with anything but wholehearted agreement, which is why it features so often in the work of those with psychic gifts.

Greener Grass

The Greener Grass element is based on the fact that we all retain some fascination with the options in life that we did *not* take. You could say they are a specific kind of Jacques Statement.

People who have always lived in congested, urban areas often yearn for what they see as the peace and freedom of a more rustic way of life. Conversely, those who have spent all their years in the countryside may long for, or be curious about, the ease, convenience and (reported) excitement of urban life. Few of us go through life without sometimes suspecting the grass is greener on the other side of the fence.

The office denizen, locked into a rather dull routine, often develops a craving for more variety, and a heightened pace of change. Conversely, the high-achieving jet-setter, rarely spending two days in the same country, may yearn for more stability and some respite from airports (and airline food), hotels and long-distance calls.

Life involves making finite choices from infinite options, and all of us are prone to wondering what would have happened if we had chosen differently. For example, suppose the client appears to have all the trappings of a successful executive career. The psychic might say something along these lines:

"I see indications of material success and professional advancement that reflect your own drive and ability to get things done. You are the sort of person who delivers results, and this characteristic has brought its rewards.

However, it has also brought its penalties. Although you seldom talk about them, I sense some feelings of a potential desire for more domestic security, and a more stable home life. I would not say this has been a serious problem for you, but I believe your loyalty to your career has not always delivered the returns you expected.

I sense that from time to time you find yourself contemplating your more domestic instincts, and wondering if they could perhaps be allowed more room to flourish. I think this has been an area of conflict within you, and I foresee that you will take steps to resolve this issue within the next 18 months or so."

Now imagine a client who comes across as a contented housewife whose every waking hour revolves around her home and family. Here is the same Greener Grass statement as before, turned on its head:

"I see indications of strong domestic instincts that have been allowed to flourish, and that have brought you a sense of security and stability. Not everyone can be a good home-maker, but you can, and you are.

However, the stability of family life has also brought its penalties. Although you seldom talk about them, I sense some feelings of a potential desire for more career progress, or at least being able to find fulfilment beyond the four walls of your home. I would not say this has been a serious problem for you, but I believe your loyalty to your home and family has not always delivered the returns you expected.

I sense that from time to time you find yourself contemplating your more professional or academic instincts, and wondering if they could perhaps be allowed more room to flourish. I think this has been an area of conflict within you, and I foresee that you will take steps to resolve this issue within the next 18 months or so."

This is precisely the same patter as before, but re-directed to flow in the right direction. Although trite in the extreme, it smacks of genuine psychic insight.

I enjoy making up Greener Grass statements and I find they work well. They are also very good for 'padding out' a thin section of a reading, since they tend to expand to anecdotal length and provide plenty of scope for improvisation.

Barnum Statement

These are artfully generalised character statements that most people will accept as reasonably accurate. Here is a selection:

> "You have a strong need for people to like and respect you."

> "You tend to feel you have a lot of unused capacity, and that people don't always give you full credit for your abilities."

> "Some of your hopes and goals tend to be pretty unrealistic."

> "You are an independent thinker and don't just accept what people tell you to believe."

The name derives from P.T. Barnum, a legendary showman who was said to have 'something to please everybody'. Barnum statements have been the subject of a number of studies conducted by psychologists. *(See Appendix note 5 for references.)*

A reading consisting solely of Barnum statements would be rather dull, but could be perfectly adequate for some situations.

I have seen more than one article in sceptical literature suggesting that cold reading consists largely of Barnum Statements. This is misleading. Barnum Statements have their uses, but they are too generalised to sustain a reading of any depth and detail.

Barnum statements and 'forking'

It is possible to get more mileage out of Barnum Statements by combining them with a technique called forking. We will look at this technique later, under Presentation, but let me briefly explain it here. Take this simple Barnum Statement:

> "You tend to be quite self-critical."

If the client seems broadly in agreement with this, the psychic can develop and strengthen the idea:

> "You often give yourself quite a hard time over mistakes that perhaps other people wouldn't worry about. You have a tendency to be your own worst enemy in this regard, and this self-critical side to your character has held you back on more than one occasion."

On the other hand, if the client seems to reject the initial statement, the psychic can develop the *same* theme in the *opposite* direction, like this:

"But this tendency is one you have learned to overcome, and these days it rarely comes to the fore. You have learned to accept yourself and your own mix of gifts and talents. You know how damaging it can be to be too self-critical, and all credit to you for having matured past the self-critical stage."

The psychic can follow two different paths, like a fork in the road. After each Barnum Statement, she can either go one way to strengthen the basic idea or go another way to reverse it. This is one way to make the humble Barnum Statement seem a little more sophisticated.

Progress Review

This concludes the first group of elements, which concerned character and personality. Now we can move on to the second group, concerning facts and events in the client's life.

Elements about facts and events

These elements chiefly concern facts (such as names and numbers) that mean something to the client, and events in the client's past. Elements that deal with future events are dealt with separately later on).

Fuzzy Fact

A Fuzzy Fact is an apparently factual statement formulated so that it (a) is quite likely to be accepted and (b) leaves plenty of scope to be developed into something more specific. Let us consider some typical examples.

Geographical

This example could be part of a tarot reading taking place somewhere in the United States:

> "I can see a connection with Europe, possibly Britain, or it could be the warmer, Mediterranean part."

The idea is to specify a large, distant part of the world with which the client may have a connection. Note that the psychic has not said whether this link is social, romantic or professional. She has not specified any particular part of Europe, which is a vast place, nor has she said if the connection is current, past or future.

However, if the client has *any connection at all* with the named part of the world, no matter how vague, she can be encouraged to supply some details. For instance, she might say:

> *"Could that include Scotland?"*

> "The link I'm getting has a sort of a Celtic flavour to it, but I wasn't sure, I'm getting Edinburgh for some reason..."

> *"There is a link on my father's side. His family comes from Scotland but it's not Edinburgh."*

> "Well, maybe that's just a place that he or his family visited once or twice, but I'm definitely getting a link with that part of the world. A connection by blood and by marriage is indicated, so that makes sense to you does it?"

> *"Yes, definitely."*

Thus the psychic shapes the initial vagueness into something much more specific. This is not just useful during the reading itself. It also affects how the reading is remembered afterwards.

A statement such as this:

> "I can see a connection with Europe, possibly Britain, or it could be the warmer, Mediterranean part."

can become mis-remembered like this:

> "I see a family connection, on your father's side, with Scotland, maybe Perthshire."

Obviously, the mis-remembered version is far more impressive than what the psychic actually said during the reading. Non-believers are often challenged to explain how a psychic could possibly have come up with some impressively accurate piece of information. Of course, it is the mis-remembered and very specific version that gets offered for analysis, not the original Fuzzy Fact.

Medical

This particular version of the Fuzzy Fact is often found in spiritualist readings. For example, if the medium is pretending to receive information about how someone passed into spirit (died), she might say something like this:

> "The gentleman with me now is telling me about a problem around the chest area, it could be sort of here (gestures vaguely towards heart and lungs)."

This could well be correct, since many people die of causes related to the heart and lungs. However, the chances of a hit are even better than they first appear. For example, if the person died from kidney failure, the psychic could claim (legitimately) that this obviously affected circulation, which is related to the functioning of the heart. Hence the initial statement is interpreted to be at least as right as it is wrong.

This particular version of the Fuzzy Fact can be developed in other ways. If the client claims this reference to the chest area is wrong, the psychic could say:

> "Oh, that's strange because the chest area is the clear impression I'm getting. How did he pass, my dear?"

> *"It was a car accident. He was killed instantly."*

> "Ah yes, I see now. What he's saying to me is that the accident triggered a heart attack a few seconds before he passed over."

Once again, the psychic wins.

Many psychics give readings that incorporate a degree of health diagnosis, even if this is not their main focus. For example, a graphologist or a tarot reader might well say:

> "Turning to the area of health, I won't dwell on the matter but I sense a bit of back trouble now and again?"

As is commonly known, the great majority of people experience *some* sort of back problem at *some* point in their lives. The back is a large part of the body, and since problems can arise in relation to the spine itself, the muscles or the skin, there is plenty of scope for a hit.

Related to events

Yet another version of the Fuzzy Fact relates to events. Here is an example that might form part of an astrological reading:

> "There's an indication here of a career in progress, or in transition. This could be your career, or it could be someone else's career that affects you."

This bears the twin hallmarks of the Fuzzy Fact: it is quite likely to be right, and it leaves scope for refinement into something more specific. The psychic does not say what is meant by 'progress' or 'transition'. It could mean getting a job, losing a job, promotion, relocation to a new office, a pay rise, a change of responsibilities, getting a new client... all sorts of things. Even the *possibility* of any of these things will count as a hit. They do not actually need to have happened.

Given that the psychic says this could refer to either the client or someone she knows, it stands a very high chance of being counted as a hit.

Another common example that often features in the spiritualist repertoire is the 'uniform'. With reference to some late member of the family, the gifted medium might say:

> "I'm getting a link with a uniform of some kind. Does this make sense to you?"

Many people have jobs that involve wearing a uniform, or wearing something that is *effectively* a uniform in the context of their work (such as the executive's smart suit, or the butcher's apron). If the deceased belongs to this category, it's a hit!

Moreover, many people who do not wear a uniform themselves work in places where others do. The potential for success does not end there. Many people have served in the armed forces at some point, providing yet more scope for a potential miracle. If all else fails, the psychic can say she is tuning in to the deceased's school days (when they may have worn a uniform) or youthful years (when they may have been into sports and worn team colours that were a sort of uniform).

I have dwelt at length on the Fuzzy Fact because it is a very versatile element that features in many different kinds of readings. It can be used to generate statements about relationships, family, career, names (of people, places or events), sets of initials, numbers, trips, holidays and celebrations.

The widespread use of the Fuzzy Fact has given rise to the common misconception that cold reading consists of vague statements. It bears repeating that it is not just vagueness that makes this element work. It is the high likelihood of the statement being right *in some way*, and the scope it offers for refinement into something more precise.

By its very nature, this element is mostly applicable to interactive readings. However, it can be used in printed or postal readings, in which case the client herself has to do all the work of finding a way to make the statement fit. Fortunately for the psychic industry, many clients are happy to oblige.

Good Chance Guess

This element involves making a guess that stands a higher chance of being right than you might think. (It is distinct from the outright fluke, or Lucky Guess, which we will look at next).

Consider this example:

> "The house where you live — is there a 2 in the number?"

This sounds like an outright guess, and in some ways it is. However, the odds of the psychic being right are higher than you might think. The majority of clients lack either the mathematical sophistication, or inclination, to work out the correct odds.

Let us investigate this a little more closely. Imagine a street with 100 houses, 50 on either side. How many houses have a 2 in their number? The answer is on the next page, but have a guess before you look.

* (pause for thought) *

The correct answer is 19, very close to one fifth of all the houses in the street. So the psychic has almost a 1 in 5 chance of being right. (The probability increases for streets with more than 19 houses but significantly fewer than 100, which in practice applies to a high proportion of streets.)

Good though this is, there is plenty more honey in the pot. If the client rejects this initial offering, the psychic might try widening it just slightly, like this:

> "Oh, that's strange because I'm definitely seeing this number 2.
> Perhaps it's the house next door?"

If we go back to our imaginary street of 100 houses, 20 of them (not among the 19 counted so far) are adjacent to a house with a 2 in the number. Therefore the psychic would get a hit if the client lived at any one of 19 + 20 houses, which is 39 in all. The possibilities do not end there. If the 'house next door' ploy has not worked, the psychic can always add this:

> "...or maybe it's the house you see opposite every morning."

This adds 8 more houses to those not counted so far. This makes a grand total of 47 houses, or almost a 50% chance of getting a hit! (If it is still a miss, the psychic uses one of the escape routes we will see later in 'The Win–Win Game'.)

The blue car

Here is another common example of a Good Chance Guess:

> "And for some reason I'm seeing a blue car outside your door."

This combines pure guesswork with intelligent thinking. The chances of getting a hit are higher than they may appear. If the client owns a blue car, it is a hit. If she has ever done so, it is a hit about her past. With a little refinement, the psychic can get a hit if any of the client's close friends or neighbours have a blue car. If the client was recently visited by any trade or professional people in a blue car or van, that also counts as a hit. There are many possibilities of getting a hit or near-hit.

The other crafty part of this guess is the choice of colour. Cars come in many colours, but in my part of the world blue is probably the most common of all. What is more, the term 'blue' covers a greater possible range of shades and hues than any other possible choice — from the deep, dark shades of Royal Blue to light cyan and intermediate shades such as aquamarine and turquoise.

I'm told that in other parts of the world the commonest colours are white, near white or shades of grey and silver. I would not be entirely surprised to learn that in these territories psychic impressions about cars tend to feature white-ish, silvery vehicles rather than blue ones.

There are many other statements that work in the same way as these two examples. Technically, they are guesses that can be right or wrong, but in fact they stand a very good chance of being right. It is also worth pointing out that in most contexts, the clients will have little or no time to analyse the subtlety involved.

Lucky Guess

The Lucky Guess element, as its name implies, is a pure guess lacking the subtlety of the 'Good Chance Guess' explained above. The psychic simply offers a name, set of initials, date or place and sees if the client accepts it.

If it is a hit, it seems miraculous and will be sure to impress the client. What's more, it can be used afterwards to give sceptics a thump since it is apparently inexplicable. If it is not a hit, the psychic can easily move on to something else (see 'The Win–Game' later).

Although there is nothing subtle about this element, I had to include it since it is so useful in cold reading terms. It is also worth emphasising that many clients apply great latitude when interpreting the psychic's offerings. Take an example like this:

> "The name Jane means something to you. I can see someone you have known quite a while, with blonde hair."

The psychic is simply guessing. However, she has not said how this name relates to the client, so more or less any connection will do. 'Jane' could be a relative, colleague or friend. She could be alive or dead, known well or only distantly, linked with the present or the past. There are many ways this could be a hit.

If the client knows a Jean, Jenny, Janet, Joanne or someone whose name sounds close, she may well offer the mild correction and credit the psychic with a near-miss. This close-sounding name could be a first name, surname ('Jones') or a nick name. It could be male or female ('Jan' and 'Juan' are common male name in some countries). Given the interpretative latitude that psychics enjoy, it is clear that a Lucky Guess stands at least a fair chance of eventually being considered a hit or a near-hit.

The three-part guess

It is also worth pointing out that if a guess has two or three parts, the client is likely to pay attention only to those parts that are correct. In the example given above, the guess contains three parts: 'Jane', 'known a long time' and 'blonde hair'. If the client has recently met a Jane with blonde hair, this will be considered a remarkable display of psychic divination. The inaccurate part (about having known her a long time) will just be ignored.

Here is another example of a three-part Lucky Guess:

> "Now for some reason I'm seeing significance with the end of August, around the twenty-sixth or a date close to that, and a man, related to you, who wears glasses."

If the client is married to a bespectacled man whose birthday is August 27th, the psychic will be credited with astounding powers that science is powerless to explain. However, the guess affords plenty of scope for at least partial success.

Any significant date from the 20th of August onwards would count as a hit. It could refer to a birthday, an anniversary, a holiday, a social function or an important decision. It could be significant every year, or just last year or just this year. It could be significant personally, socially or professionally.

The man could be a husband, partner, brother, relative, friend, colleague or a professional contact (such as the client's doctor, accountant or garage mechanic). He could be someone the client has known for years, or met once. Alive or dead, near or far, well-known or a distant acquaintance. The more possibilities you become aware of, the more chances you see for the Lucky Guess to be considered a hit.

Of course, the more Lucky Guesses the psychic includes, the higher her chances of getting a hit somewhere along the line. Some psychics manage to mention dozens of different names, sets of initials, dates or places in a single reading. The hits get talked about afterwards and the misses get forgotten.

Habitual guessing

I should just add that many cold readers get into the habit of using Lucky Guesses even when not giving readings. For example, when chatting to someone for the first time they may casually guess that person's star sign, or a relative's name, or a particular hobby. It is no crime to be wrong, and the psychic can always say she spoke before she had developed proper rapport.

On the other hand, if the Lucky Guess happens to be right then it becomes the stuff of legend.

On one occasion I was talking to a TV researcher on the phone. I made some mild joke about her being 'highly efficient, a typical Sagittarius'. As it happened, her star sign *was* Sagittarius and she was highly impressed. Throughout my involvement with this particular TV crew, the researcher never tired of recycling this tale of my astounding powers. I have shown salesmen how to use similar approaches to make friends with 'chilly' receptionists who may be unhelpfully good at blocking access to strong prospects.

Stat Fact

Stat Facts are statements based on statistics and demographic data. There is a wealth of such information available, from libraries, specialist publications, commercial databases and the internet.

This kind of information can be very useful to psychics. For example, imagine a psychic is giving readings in a region where, statistically, most of the women who have part-time jobs work either in the health services or the textile industry. If the psychic has reason to think her client works part-time, she knows which two trades are most likely to be worth mentioning. As with many aspects of cold reading, there are good and bad ways of using this information. Here is the bad way:

> "There is an indication that your career is related to health. Or possibly textiles."

This is as transparent as it is trite. In contrast, imagine the psychic is giving an astrological reading and weaves her spell like this:

> "Looking at career influences, the presence of Aries suggests that you have a great capacity for working with people and helping them. In fact the conjunctions of your fifth house suggest you could be very successful if you were working with people who needed care or counselling, in one form or another. The stars suggest that this could be right for you..."

At this point, the psychic pauses to see if the client seems to be agreeing. If not, the psychic changes tack:

> "...but that's more to do with your potential, rather than your actual occupation. The influence of Saturn at the moment, coupled with your Capricorn nature, suggests you may have found your energy directed towards manual work of a skilled nature. Does this make sense to you?"

In this way, the psychic can mention two likely careers, health and textiles, in a way that sounds like the information is coming from the stars rather than local census statistics.

Obviously, the success of this element depends on how reliable the information is and how intelligently it is applied. Experienced cold readers make it their business to gather information that is likely to prove useful. Mediums and spiritualists, for example, have everything to gain from learning the statistically commonest causes of death, and to flavour their Stat Fact statements accordingly.

There is certainly no shortage of demographic data available. There are tables and reports pertaining to educational attainment, careers, salary levels, marrying age, prevailing health problems and myriad other subjects.

To rely on very well-known statistics is to invite unimpressed and rather cynical responses. However, less well-known statistics can be extremely useful, as can attention to fine distinctions. For example, what is the most popular sport or pastime in Britain? Most British people would say football, which is true in terms of the numbers who have an interest *as spectators*. But in terms of those who *actively take part*, the top sport is angling or fishing. Similarly, few of my fellow Brits would guess that *doing jig-saw puzzles* is something like the fifth most popular recreational pursuit in the country.

Trivia Stat

This element consists of a statement about trivial domestic and personal details. Whereas the Stat Fact is derived from official statistics, Trivia Stats are based on nothing more than experience of life. Cold readers develop their own favourite Trivia Stats over time. Here are a few I have collected over the years. See what you think!

Regarding items found around the home

- a box of old photographs somewhere, not neatly sorted into albums

- some old medicine or medical supplies years out of date

- at least one toy, or some books, that are mementoes from childhood

- some item of jewellery, or maybe war medals, from a deceased family member
- a pack of cards, even if they say they never play cards, often with one or more cards missing
- some electronic gizmo or gadget that no longer works and will never be repaired, but has not been thrown out
- a notepad or message board that once had a matching pen but the pen is now missing
- a note, attached to the fridge or near a phone or a desk, that is significantly out of date
- a few books or some paraphernalia associated with a hobby or interest that is no longer pursued
- a calendar that has nothing to do with the current year
- consecutive issues of a magazine once subscribed to but no longer
- a drawer that does not slide as easily as it should, or a cabinet with doors or hinges that do not work properly
- some item on open display that was bought on holiday
- a key that is now redundant, or the exact purpose of which has been forgotten
- a broken watch or clock

Regarding men and women:

- most men tried learning a musical instrument as a child, but then gave up
- most men wore a moustache or beard at some point, even if they have been clean-shaven for years
- most men have at least one old suit hanging in their wardrobe that they can no longer fit into
- most women own, or have owned, an item of clothing that they bought and then never wore
- most women have many more pairs of shoes than they actually need in strictly practical terms
- most women keep photos of their loved ones in their purse or otherwise near them, even if they are not the sentimental type

- most women wear their hair long as a child, then adopt a shorter haircut when they get older
- most women have at least one ear-ring the partner of which is missing presumed lost
- most people have, or have had, a scar on the left knee
- most people have a number '2' in their house number, or know someone who does
- most people will have been involved in some sort of childhood accident that involved water
- most people with fair skin have experienced bad sunburn at least once

To state the obvious, worthwhile Trivia Stats vary according to culture, region and context. The psychic who wants to use this element has to acquire examples appropriate to her region and clientele. The same is true for many other cold reading elements.

Theme and variations

Trivia Stats can be woven into almost any kind of psychic reading if given a little presentational embellishment. For example, it is no good simply announcing:

"You have a box of old photographs at home."

This lacks presentational flair, even if it happens to be correct. Here's a much better version:

"Ah... the 3 of Swords and, in the same line, The World. A very interesting combination. In general, The World pertains to your own personal domain, such as your own home or your own room. This combination suggests the sort of person who makes clear distinctions between what's important and what isn't. You're quite analytical in this respect. You might be the sort who has some photographs, the important ones, neatly compiled into albums, and others that you just sling into an old box, any old how, and never look at."

Here is how the palmistry version might go:

"This line at the base of the ring finger indicates your materialistic nature. It's clearly bisected by the heart line, indicating a person who makes clear distinctions. You treasure some possessions like gold dust, while you're happy to discard others as if they don't matter. You know the sort of thing I mean, like people who have loads of family photos: some are neatly pasted into albums kept in the living room while others get slung in a box in a cupboard in the bedroom."

Personally, I have used the Trivia Stat very little. Other cold readers seem to set great store by their collection of such statements. As with so many other aspects of cold reading, it is purely a matter of personal style, preference and experience.

Cultural Trend

This is closely allied to the Stat Fact and the Trivia Stat. It is simply based on observing prevailing social and cultural trends, and extrapolating from them. A good knowledge of current trends can help the psychic to make plausible statements about the client's present-day life, including her character, attitudes, pastimes and pre-occupations. Educated guesses about how these trends will develop can help the psychic formulate predictions for the client's near future (in addition to all the elements about future events discussed later in this book).

After I published the first edition of this book, I received feedback from a great many people. One in particular, whom I met after a lecture in Los Angeles, is blessed with very sharp insight and a good sense of fun. For various reasons, he wishes only to be known as Shallow Larynx. On the subject of Cultural Trends, Shallow Larynx sent me this summary. I thought I would share it with you in more or less un-retouched form. It was first written around 2002 which is why some aspects may seem a little dated.

Shallow Larynx on Cultural Trends

I can tell you a few trends I have noticed. Wealthy men are picking up the appearance paranoia once reserved for their sisters. Men's skin care products are a $35 million industry and growing. They include moisturisers, under-eye cream and exfoliant (but done in a manly way).

It is common for professional men to get manicures. I know of one premier 5-star spa located in California. They hold 'Men's Week' four or five times a year. A week at this spa rarely costs less than $5000. Men's Weeks are *always* sold out well in advance.

Men are really catching up on plastic surgery too. I spoke to a woman who runs a boutique hotel in Beverly Hills. This boutique opened its doors in 1988. The proprietor tells me she has seen bookings among male patients jump from 6 percent to 25 percent in the last few years.

Of course, the big imperative for men is exactly the same as that for women. If I remember right, the most popular male procedure is a facelift, with liposuction not far behind. Men tend to go for it round 40 or so, and the motive is defending one's perceived market value. All worth knowing, if you are cold reader and your client is a man who sports a manicure, looks suspiciously healthy, and seems younger than his years.

Houses are getting bigger. I remember reading somewhere that the average luxury house has doubled in square footage size. This made me think of real estate data, which can be a goldmine of information. There are websites where you can enter any zip code and get detailed information on a community.

On the same lines, there is a web site for 'Who's Who in Luxury Real Estate'. This is a members-only association of luxury real estate brokers who have to earn their way in. It is international. They have a broker search engine on their site, and many of the brokers have web pages, which might prove useful.

Returning to the subject of housing, it is becoming more common to buy a plot of land, tear down the existing, perfectly good house and build a new one. This is called a 'teardown', unsurprisingly.

The internet has changed the way people live. Now, you can work from home much more easily. This means that what would have been a resort home or vacation home is now home, period. Resort communities, like Aspen and Palm Beach, are becoming year-round places to live. And what about the trends in luxury homes? These days it is almost a given that the following rooms are part of the house: his and hers bathrooms, home office, home gym, home theatre or 'entertainment centre'.

Kitchens have changed. They used to be purely a service area at the back of the house. Now, the kitchen has become a sort of showpiece, placed up the front of the house and suitable for hosting guests. It may have a 6000 dollar pizza oven, working beer taps, you name it. It is somewhat analogous to what I call the 'SUV effect'. You sure as hell do not *need* it, but you certainly *want* it, and it is 'chic' to have it.

(Editorial note for the uninitiated: an 'SUV' is a Sport Utility Vehicle. This is a large and very bulky block of car-shaped metal featuring a high wheel-base, such that you may need a small stepladder to get in or out. They come equipped with a vast array of design features and accessories well-suited to shooting big game or embarking on a personal quest to discover the source of the Nile. Over the past decade, these have proved staggeringly popular with people whose most exotic intention is to drive down to the beauty parlour or pick kids up from school – I.R.)

Cooking used to be a chore. Now, it is a status symbol. Showing off your $125 balsamic vinegars, imported Scottish game hens and huge trophy kitchen is just another way of advertising how wealthy you are. The up-market kitchen supplies industry has really taken off in recent years.

Speaking of SUVs, they are far more popular than sports cars. People who buy them routinely take them in to have extra features added. Of course, status symbol sports cars are still with us. But there are many high-flying business executives these days who want their rental car to be an SUV.

It is very, very common for teenage girls to shoplift something before they reach womanhood. Some make it into a competitive sport. Frustrated teenage boys who act out criminally tend to choose violence. Frustrated teenage girls steal stuff — usually items that are small but expensive. There is a store in my local mall that is clearly aimed at the 12–18 crowd. It has a big poster on the wall showing a girl in a white angel costume. She is shrugging her shoulders. Her gown has a big ugly green stain on it. The poster says, 'Don't Stain Your Perfect Reputation. We Prosecute Shoplifters.'

End of report from Shallow Larynx

My sincere thanks to Shallow Larynx for this rich seam of observations. There is little for me to add. The Psychic who wishes to capitalise upon this kind of element strives to match this kind of awareness, noticing not only the trends themselves but their roots, causes and implications.

Childhood Memory

As its name implies, this element consists of a character statement based on common experiences of childhood. The trick is to devise statements that are only slightly less than obvious, or at least seem to be so in the context of a reading. One of my personal favourites is 'The abandoned interest':

> "In your younger years I get the impression of a particular interest or subject you were very keen on, where you showed lots of promise. I get a feeling that this was something on the creative or artistic side, where perhaps your parents felt you might go on to great things, but it was not to be."

This kind of comment will win agreement from most clients. The simple fact is that most children pursue their strongest aptitudes with great enthusiasm. However, they generally fail to develop their personal passions into fame and fortune, and so these interests become neglected or abandoned.

The interest generally falls into one of two categories: either creative–artistic or sports–athletics. When I use this element, I make a guess as to which of the two (creative or sporty) I think is more likely. This is often not too difficult as many people who are fit and active in early life are inclined to stay that way. If I guess wrong I can try offering the alternative.

Assuming I do guess correctly, I can try to get a more specific hit just by knowing the commonest choices. On the creative side, the most likely choice is music followed by art, writing and dancing. On the sports side, the commonest example is involvement in some sort of team sport, followed by swimming, running and one of the martial arts.

Words and significance

In case the Childhood Memory seems too simple to be effective, let me mention another aspect of cold reading psychology. During a successful reading, the psychic may provide most of the *words* but the client provides the *significance*. Clients tend to graft their own specific experiences on to the more generalised words and themes provided by the psychic.

This is an important psychological factor in cold reading. It applies to the majority of elements listed in this section, but it is especially relevant to the Childhood Memory. The psychic's simple reference to 'a talent or ability' can evoke a vivid set of memories in the client's mind: striving to master the piano, producing a first oil painting, winning an athletics prize and so on. Subsequently, the psychic gets the credit not for the simple Childhood Memory statement in its raw form, but for having 'perceived' specific and heartfelt memories of years gone by.

The anxious parents

Another Childhood Memory that I have used with great success is 'The anxious parents', which goes like this:

> "Going back to your younger years, while all children have a few minor illnesses I can sense something more significant. It may have been an illness, it could have been an injury or an accident, but it was quite serious. I sense your parents and others around you were more worried at the time than they needed to be, given that things turned out okay."

This is only one step removed from the obvious (all children go through some illness and disease) to something slightly less obvious (most children experience at least one serious illness or accidental injury). Appearing to 'see' the scene, and to respond to the emotions at the time, lends the statement a nice psychic flavour. A very similar variant is the 'accident involving water'. Most people can find something in their childhood that ties in with a statement along these lines.

The lucky job

Another Childhood Memory statement that I have used refers to early career steps rather than childhood. I call it 'The lucky job':

> "I'm looking at the time when you got your first serious job or made your first career move. I sense that there was something lucky about it, maybe a strong coincidence or a fluke in your favour, something unusual about how you came to get this job or this position. I think perhaps this makes sense to you."

This is just another example of the same Childhood Memory formula: a very common growing-up experience described in a slightly less than obvious way. Employers generally look for experience, and young people cannot gain experience until someone gives them a job. Nine times out of ten, this vicious circle only gets broken through sheer luck or a surprising opportunity. There is nothing remarkable about this, but it falls into the category of 'slightly less than obvious', especially in the context of a psychic reading.

Folk Wisdom

Psychics are no enemies of tired cliché. Many readings are littered with that combination of an appeal to common experience and boundless optimism that passes for folk-wisdom. Here are a few examples:

> "After this past year, it's not surprising you need a break. Let's face it, we all need a little breathing space now and again to re-charge our batteries."

> "We all need to talk things over with a friend from time to time, and it's as true now as it ever was: two heads really are better than one."

> "The main thing is not to worry. Let's be honest, these things often have a way of coming right in the end one way or another, and then you look back and you think well, what was all the worry about?"

> "There's quite definitely light at the end of the tunnel. As the old saying has it, the sky is always darkest just before the dawn."

> "This challenge may seem a little daunting, but then again it's surprising what you can do when you put your mind to it, isn't it?"

This is not a particularly useful element, but it can be useful for padding out a reading or bringing one section to a neat coda before moving on to something else.

This element ties in with a Presentation point called 'Keeping it folksy' which we will come to later.

Seasonal Touch

The Seasonal Touch is a very simple element. The psychic merely offers statements based on the time of year or other seasonal factors. These obviously vary according to the country, culture and society in which the psychic is giving the reading, but it is nonetheless a very useful element.

For example, I live in England where the season of spring is often associated with so-called 'spring cleaning' and embarking on major new DIY tasks around the home. January and July are the commonest months for major sales in the shops, which many women will flock to in search of bargains.

The financial calendar can also prove useful. One of my correspondents in the United States tells me that between the months of January and April many people will have federal income taxes on their mind.

To get the most out of this element, give some thought to how many different 'calendars' we all live by. I have already referred to three, which we might call the household calendar, the retail calendar and the financial calendar. There are many others: the sports calendar, the entertainment industry calendar (seasons for hot new shows or dreary old repeats), the culinary calendar and so on. Each of these can lend itself to a good Seasonal Touch element.

Adding imagery

One way to improve this element is to add appropriate imagery. For instance, this is not so good:

> "I sense you have been doing some major cleaning chores around the home."

This is better:

> "If I focus for a moment on the domestic aspect of life, I'm getting
> impressions of activity and quite a lot of effort. In fact I'd even
> describe it as stress and strain. I mean that in both the physical sense,
> perhaps one or aches down your back, and the emotional sense of
> trying to sort out clutter and impose some sense of order on your
> environment. I'm sensing that you have a very energetic aura, but
> recently you have known some fatigue as well."

Extrapolation

Statements derived from basic seasonal data do not have to
sound trite and obvious. Psychics can extrapolate from the data
in order to make observations that sound full of inspired wisdom
and insight.

If many women go to big discount sales in July, then many of
them will face hefty credit card bills about a month later and may
go on an economy drive the month after that. Hence the psychic
giving a reading in September, provided the client seems likely to
fit this pattern, can discuss domestic financial affairs with some
confidence.

Different views

Another way to squeeze more juice out of the Seasonal Touch is
to think about different points of view. Consider the example
mentioned above of July being a time when many women go to
discount sales in search of bargains. Consider four different
people:

- the keen bargain-hunter, who relishes the sales

- the shop assistant, who dreads the extra workload and
  general upheaval

- the husband, who is rather shocked at the impact on the
  marital credit card

- someone who has no interest in the sales and resents the
  disruption in their favourite shops and stores

Four different people, with four very different perspectives. Hence
one piece of information can provide very different material for
readings depending on which of these four people turns up for a
reading. Of course, 'none of the above' is also a possibility, in
which case the psychic will just have to talk about something else.

Psychics can also dream up Seasonal Touch statements that are more likely to apply to men than women. Sporting fixtures provide one obvious source of material. In England, where I live, quite a few men would regard the start or climax of various sports seasons as their main reason for living. Some find it easier to recite a string of soccer statistics than to name their wife's birthday or, in extreme cases, their wife.

The psychic will generally find these enthusiasts easy to recognise. For example, it is not hard to identify English soccer enthusiasts. The prominent eyebrow ridge, trailing knuckles and ongoing quest for the secret of fire are highly reliable indicators. Indeed, many are recognisable from security camera and news footage gathered at various European football stadiums, or town centres that have the grave misfortune to be nearby.

Opposites Game

The Opposites Game is a very intriguing element, and one that fascinated me when I first came across it.

The psychic suggests to the client that there is someone in her life whom she does not get along with, or with whom she feels some rather unwelcome friction or tension. The psychic then proceeds to describe this 'awkward' or 'unhelpful' person in some detail. This is quite a remarkable thing to be able to do.

So how is this psychic miracle achieved? The answer is that the psychic simply describes the exact *opposite* of the client herself! If the client seems quite reserved and formal, the psychic describes someone who seems carefree, casual and extrovert. If the client seems rather authoritative and outspoken, the psychic describes someone timid and shy. If the client seems rather dry and lacking in humour, the psychic describes someone full of fun and practical jokes. In this way, the psychic can deliver what seems like quite a highly impressive 'psychic profile' of this shadowy enemy figure.

More often than not, the client will be able to identify *someone* who matches the description, and whom she dislikes to *some* extent. This element is clearly less than sure-fire, and it is one that I have very little experience of using. Nonetheless, it is mentioned by more than one source on cold reading and is therefore probably worth trying.

Push Statement

I have deliberately saved the Push Statement until last in this section. It is the hardest element to explain clearly, but also one of the most powerful.

The elements I have listed so far are intended to be *accepted* by the client. The psychic is hoping the client will say her statements are accurate or at least plausible.

Push Statements are quite different. They are intentionally designed to be *rejected* by the client. More specifically, to be rejected *at first*. However, they can almost always be made to fit if the psychic pushes with sufficient confidence and, at the same time, subtly expands the scope for agreement.

Push statements are hard to make up and generally evolve with experience over many readings. I only have one or two that I trust, and I use them sparingly. One that I have used quite a lot is 'The red floor'. It goes something like this:

> "About three months ago, I see you standing in a room of some kind. It seems a strange detail to mention, but I see a red or red-ish floor. I don't think it's your home or where you work. It's somewhere else. There's this red colour around you, and this is a place of some significance to you. Now I can only tell you what I'm getting, whether or not it makes sense, and I feel you went to this place for a meeting of some kind. I don't know if there's one other person involved or a group, but someone's expecting you to be there, and you're having to wait for them."

This almost always gets a negative response from the client, which is what I would expect. I then begin to push the statement and appear highly confident that the meaning will become clear eventually. This sense of confidence is important, and subtly places the onus on the client to find something that matches.

As I continue to push my initial statement, I start to subtly include more options. The colour might have been a kind of rusty brown, or an autumnal shade. It might not have been actually the floor that was significant, so much as the general environment that had a red-ish colour scheme, or a danger zone (red = danger). The meeting could have been intentional or accidental, significant or trivial, routine or a one-off. It could have been social, professional, family or romantic.

Sooner or later, in a very high percentage of cases, the client will remember *something* that fits. The whole point of a Push Statement is that the psychic seems aware of something *that the client herself had forgotten*. This is devastatingly impressive when it works. It is one thing for a psychic to detect things the client is aware of. It is quite another for the psychic to apparently 'see' things the client herself had more or less forgotten.

It is not easy to devise good Push Statements. The details have to be just sufficiently unusual to lie beyond guesswork, but just sufficiently common to stand a chance of being right. The details must also be ones that the psychic can expand and re-interpret in progressively broader terms as the psychic 'helps' the client to remember something that matches.

The shoe and the party

Another example is 'The shoe and the party', which I have used more than once on female clients aged under 35. It goes like this:

> "I'm getting the impression of a party or celebration that I think took place around Christmas time, but not necessarily an actual Christmas party. There's a car involved, and a problem with this car or with transportation. I can see you holding a shoe, or having problems with one of your shoes. It could be something common, like a broken heel, or something more unusual. Maybe it was a strap that had broken or caught in something. I see you in a bit of a bad mood about it, and telling other people. Is this making sense?"

Naturally, this element can sometimes lead nowhere. In the face of persistent rejection an escape tunnel is needed. One good option is to say that if the event being referred to has not happened yet then it will do soon. Another is to invite the client to carry on trying to think back, because the meaning may come to her later. Other ways of escaping from misses are covered later in 'The Win–Win Game'.

A successful push

I was once demonstrating cold reading in a TV production meeting. In the course of a reading for one of the production assistants, I used 'the shoe and the party' and added the name 'James'. She was unable to find any match.

Ten minutes after I had *ended* the reading, and while I was in conversation with someone else, the girl suddenly became very excited. In tones of sheer disbelief, she exclaimed that she had just remembered a party from her teenage years during which she had indeed broken her shoe while dancing with a friend called James! Although this was by no means a complete success, the girl simply could not believe that I had managed to 'perceive' this long-distant event so accurately.

I have had my successes and failures with Push Statements, but on balance I believe they are worthwhile.

Progress Review

This concludes the second group of elements, which concerned facts and events. The first two groups we have looked at involve giving the client information, or at least appearing to do so. However, a large part of cold reading is concerned with *extracting* information, rather than supplying it. This is the theme of the next group of elements.

Elements about extracting information

The following elements provide ways of obtaining information from the client and then putting it to good use. In essence, they involve getting information simply by asking for it. Although this sounds very blatant, the psychic can disguise this process extremely well *if she has to*. In fact, the client may feel she never gave the psychic any information at all.

Direct Question

I will begin with the simplest and most transparent approach. In the case of the Direct Question, the psychic simply asks for the information she wants, like this:

"Tell me, what is it that's on your mind?"

Or like this:

"Most of the people who come to see me have something that has been weighing heavily on their heart, perhaps an area of life where they are looking for some answers and some light at the end of the tunnel. What would this be in your case?"

This may seem too facile to be part of the cold reading process, but it all depends on the client's attitude. Many clients are pre-committed. They trust the psychic and the belief system, and neither seek nor require any 'proof' of the psychic's gifts. Their view is that they want help, the psychic is there to provide it, and the sooner they can get down to details the better.

If the psychic knows she is dealing with this kind of client, she may use opening lines that openly acknowledge this situation. A seductive reference to the notion of 'value for money' can also help. It might go something like this:

"How we use this session is entirely up to you. If you like, I could take my time and try to sense the areas you want me to talk about and the specific problem that has brought you here today. I'm happy to do it this way. However, on occasion it can take me a while. The other way is that you just tell me what's on your mind and we can get off to a flying start. I'm here to listen, and I do want to help you."

Delivered to a suitably uncritical and pre-committed client, this kind of pitch will coax forth all the information the psychic could possibly use. In extreme cases, the psychic's toughest problem may be to stem the outpouring of personal information long enough to get the reading started.

Direct Questions are most often used at the start of the reading, to establish an appropriate focus. However, if the client is sufficiently uncritical and receptive to this kind of blatant inquisition, then the psychic is free to use Direct Questions throughout the reading:

"Tell me, are you currently in a long-term relationship, or not?"

"Are you satisfied in terms of your career, or is there a problem?"

"Who has passed over that you want to try and contact today?"

So much for the artless Direct Question and readings that rely on it. Most clients are a little more discerning than this and hence psychics use rather more subtle ways to extract information.

Incidental Question

Incidental Questions take the form of small conversational phrases tacked on to the end of longer sections of a reading. They make the request for information sound almost incidental.

There are two types of Incidental Questions. The first type are simply designed to prompt for feedback. Here is a selection:

"...now why would that be?"
"...is this making sense to you?"
"...can you relate to this?"
"...does this sound right?"
"...would you say this is along the right lines for you?"
"...this is significant to you, isn't it?"

The second type cover all the standard 'checklist' questions taught to trainee reporters and journalists: who, what, where, when, how and why. Suppose that the psychic has claimed to perceive some 'impression' or 'sign'. She might then add phrases such as these:

"...so who might this refer to please?"
"...what might this link to in your life?"
"...what period of your life, please, might this relate to?"
"...so tell me, how might this be significant to you?"

The psychic's inflection and tone of voice can make a big difference to the success of this illusion. A very casual, incidental mention of, "...now who do you think this could be?", can slip by like a ship in the night if the delivery is sufficiently smooth. A good cold reader can litter her reading with Incidental Questions yet leave the client feeling no questions were ever asked.

Veiled Question

The Veiled Question is a request for information worded to sound like a statement. The psychic acts as if she is *giving* information, when in fact she is *extracting* it.

Suppose the psychic has come to a point in the reading where she wants to ask the client whether her job involves plenty of travel. Here is how she might use a Veiled Question to sound like she is giving information rather than asking for it:

> "I'm picking up an impression here that you could be involved with work that involves a lot of travelling. I don't know if this is now or some time in the past, but that's what the cards suggest. Is this making sense to you?"

The psychic can turn almost any question into what sounds like a tentative statement. In this way, she can gather information about all manner of subjects: family, career, interests, problems, health, relationships and so on.

Disguising the illusion

In the last example, the psychic ended with an Incidental Question, "...is this making sense to you?". Some choose to disguise this element even further by adopting a slightly more confident style that avoids ever actually asking a specific question. For instance, the final part of the above example could be modified like this:

> "...I don't know if this is now or some time in the past, but that's what the cards suggest, and I feel that this is something you can relate to at this time."

This slight change of wording makes no practical difference. The psychic is still trying to extract useful feedback from the client. However, it is more deceptive in the sense that the psychic has taken care to express herself with a statement rather than a question. In the strict grammatical sense, she can legitimately claim that no questions were asked at any time. As many psychics and followers are aware, this can occasionally be useful for deflecting sceptical criticism.

Themes and variations

There are countless themes and variations on the Veiled Question. For example, in the course of an astrological reading suppose the astrologer wants to ask if the client is facing a large financial purchase, such as a car or a house. Turning this into a Veiled Question, she might say:

"Looking at the rising influence of Saturn, there's an indication here to do with money and of possible financial concern. What this seems to be about, if my interpretation is correct, is a major decision related to money or finances. What's more, it's the sort of decision that could have consequences for quite some time to come. This is making sense to you, isn't it?"

It is just as easy to pick names and other factual details out of thin air. For example, a clairvoyant might go through a few seconds of inner concentration before saying:

"The name 'Jane' is coming to me, and although I'm not sure of the link, possibly something professional rather than personal, this is a name that I believe has significance for you at this time."

This sounds like a statement, but it is really just a way of asking if the client knows anyone who is either called 'Jane' or has a name that sounds similar.

Given a sufficiently smooth and plausible delivery, the Veiled Question can create a neatly convincing illusion that the psychic has already divined some crucial information, via her amazing psychic gifts, and is just working with the client to sketch in a few fine details.

Flat tone and rising tone

As a final note on the Veiled Question, note that minor adjustments to intonation and delivery can help to disguise the fact that a question is being asked. Take this example:

"There's an impression here of a link with sport and athletics."

As you can readily demonstrate for yourself, this can be said as either a statement or a question. If you use a relatively flat and even tone, it is a statement. If you use a rising tone towards the end, it becomes a question.

Diverted Question

This element involves the psychic taking a piece of information that has already arisen during the reading and feeding it back to the client in a modified form. To see how this works, imagine that during an early part of a tarot reading the psychic uses a Direct Question like this:

"Now, just to help me interpret this correctly, do you work in teaching or a similar field?"

"No I don't."

"Okay, that's fine. What do you actually do for a living?"

"I run my own design service."

The psychic now has a piece of factual information. She continues with the reading, making *no reference at all* to this fragment of factual data. As she does so, at the back of her mind she makes some educated guesses based on this information.

Since the client is involved in design, she is probably creative and artistic. Since she has taken on the challenge of running her own business, she must be fairly self-confident and probably in good heath (people with health worries do not choose to start up their own company). She probably faces plenty of stress and long hours of work. It is also safe to assume that, like most people running small businesses, she has some clients who cause cash flow problems by not paying her on time.

The psychic can feed all of these reasonable guesses into a later part of the reading. For example, suppose that she moves on to the theme of health. It could sound like this:

"Turning to health matters, the cards suggest you have generally had little cause for concern. You have a good temperament, and may also find creative outlets for stress and tension that you find therapeutic. However, there are signs of recurring anxiety, and the presence of the Ten of Coins suggests that this may be related to finance.

This is quite interesting, since this card, the Falling Tower, guides us to reverse the normal way of looking at things. So while for the majority of people the problem is just a lack of money, your particular anxiety may be slightly different. The cards suggest a picture where there *is* money coming towards you, but it often remains tantalisingly out of your grasp for some reason."

In this example, a simple fact about the client's career provides the basis for an extended sequence about health. The clever part of this is that the psychic can honestly claim never to have asked a single question about health since the reading began!

The Diverted Question requires the psychic to *extrapolate* from a piece of information and reach some plausible conclusions. These conclusions can pertain to the same subject area (in this example 'career') or to a completely different one (in this example 'health'). The latter approach is more deceptive.

The 'sporty' client

To take another example, consider a reading is in progress. The psychic asks a Direct Question about leisure interests and the client says she likes sports and games. At the back of her mind, while she proceeds with some other aspect of the reading, the psychic can make some educated guesses based on this information.

Since the client is the 'sporty' type, it's safe to say she probably takes health issues quite seriously. She is probably disinclined to smoke, drink too much or eat junk food. Her social life is unlikely to involve many people who have these vices, or the places they go to. She is probably attracted to partners who also keep themselves in reasonably good shape — or, if they do not, she may have tried to encourage them to do so!

Keeping fit takes a lot of time and commitment. Hence the client probably has good mental discipline but may miss out on a lot of popular culture and trivia. While the couch potatoes are watching TV, she is down at the gym or enjoying a 5 mile jog. Hence she may well be less familiar than most people with the latest hit TV shows, movies and songs. She probably plans rather active and adventurous vacations for herself. Just lazing around on a beach and soaking up the sun is unlikely to appeal to her.

When this kind of educated guesswork works well, it can deliver astonishing results. It's one way for the psychic to create a very strong impression that she knows things that she could not have known via any normal means.

Of course, since it *is* educated guesswork it can go wrong and lead to the psychic offering some statements that are incorrect. However, as I have already mentioned several times, this is not a problem. More on this later, in 'The Win–Win Game'.

Jargon Blitz

The Jargon Blitz is yet another way to prompt the client for information. It consists of an explicit reference to the supposed workings of the psychic system in use, liberally peppered with appropriate jargon, culminating in a prompt for feedback.

In a tarot reading, the Jargon Blitz would involve references to the meanings of specific cards and other tarot terminology. It might sound something like this:

> "Interestingly enough, I see we've got the Five of Swords: an important card within the lesser arcana, traditionally associated with challenge and struggle in affairs of the heart. What's intriguing is that in the same conjunction of the spread, we've already had 'The Hermit', originally one of the lower triad cards and now generally regarded as indicating not only solitude but also the accomplishment of personal goals. It's as if the cards are suggesting your personal goals are, at this time, due to take priority over romance. Does this makes sense to you?"

To the best of my knowledge, 'lesser arcana' and 'the spread' (meaning the layout of the cards) are genuine pieces of tarot lore, whereas 'conjunction' and 'triad' mean nothing in the context of a tarot reading. However, they *sound* good and authoritative, which is all that matters.

In cold reading terms, the traditional meaning ascribed to each tarot card is irrelevant. A book on tarot lore may suggest that 'The Tower' signifies change in existing relationships. However, the psychic can attribute any meaning she wants to this or any other card without affecting the perceived merits of the reading. This is why the Jargon Blitz can be such fun to use. It doesn't matter whether what is said is 'accurate' in terms of traditional lore. It just has to sound convincing and lead to that all-important prompt for feedback.

In similar vein, if offering an astrological analysis the cold reader only needs a small amount of the appropriate vocabulary, such as 'trine', 'ascendant', 'fifth house' and so on, in order to make the reading sound plausible.

Some cold readers learn about the systems they are using in order to at least deploy the jargon accurately. While this knowledge can never hurt the cold reading process, I remain far from convinced that it ever helps either. In my experience, a good working knowledge of the divinatory system being used makes little difference to the effectiveness of a reading.

Whether the jargon is used in an informed way or not, the Jargon Blitz remains a highly useful element in readings. It allows the psychic to vary the way she prompts for information and strengthens the belief system in use (as mentioned earlier, in 'The Set Up'). It imposes the authority of the psychic and helps to promote a sense of ritual which, as I have already mentioned, inhibits awkward responses and promotes the desired degree of co-operation.

Vanishing Negative

This is a negative question of ambiguous tone and phrasing. Whether the client agrees or disagrees, it can be counted as a hit. Here is an example:

"Moving on to career matters, you don't work with children do you?"

"No I don't."

"No, I thought not. That's not really your role..."

Or alternatively:

"Moving on to career matters, you don't work with children do you?"

"I do actually, part-time."

"Yes, I thought so. A strong affinity with children indicated... "

The cute phrasing means that the negative part of the question simply vanishes if necessary, never to be remembered.

Re-affirm, re-assure, expand

The Vanishing Negative is very useful even in its basic form. However, there are at least three good ways to embellish it and make it seem a little more convincing.

The first is for the psychic to enhance the client's own response, and emphasise that they are in complete agreement. The second is to offer some reassuring comment that disparages the alternative option rejected by the client. The third is to expand upon the point, as if the initial question was unimportant preamble.

By way of illustration, consider this:

"At this point, I want to move on and address money and career matters. You don't work for yourself do you?"

"No I don't."

First, establish agreement:

> "No, I didn't think so. I got quite a clear impression that you weren't in that category."

Next, the reassurance and gentle disparagement:

> "I don't think you're cut out to be one of those flashy, egocentric entrepreneurs with all that stress and hassle. Most of them never get anywhere anyway!"

Finally, the expansion:

> "Anyway, the reason I sensed you work for someone else rather than working for yourself is that I see a change in your relationship with your employer..."

The psychic can continue with the reading as if she *knew* that the client was not self-employed. The fact that she asked a question to discover this fact is never noticed. Here's the alternative version:

> "At this point, I want to move on and address money and career matters. You don't work for yourself do you?"

> *"Yes, I do actually. Have done for a while."*

First, the agreement (featuring the instant Vanishing Negative):

> "Yes, I thought so. It's a clear aspect of the story the cards are telling me."

Next, the reassurance and gentle disparagement:

> "I don't think you're cut out to be just another nine-to-five wage slave. That could never be truly fulfilling for someone like you. You have too much drive and too many good ideas of your own."

Finally, the expansion:

> "The reason I picked up on the fact that you run your own business is that I foresee some very good prospects in the near future... "

The simple Vanishing Negative scores another hit for the gifted psychic!

Sherlock Strategy

This element consists of extracting information from visual clues. In a previous section ('Popular Misconceptions') I said I regard this technique as far more limited in scope than some sources suggest. Nonetheless, it certainly has a part to play.

As is usually the case with cold reading elements, the way the information is used is often more important than how it is derived. For example, if the client has long, even nails on her right hand and very short nails on her left, the psychic can deduce that she probably plays the guitar. (If the nails are the other way around, she probably plays the guitar and is also left-handed!)

The weak way to use this observation is to say:

"Your astrological chart suggests you play the guitar."

The better way is to say something along these lines:

"As a Gemini with the influence of Venus in your third house, you may well be inclined to artistic self-expression. You have almost certainly felt the need to explore forms of communication and expression that go beyond the merely verbal. You have access to sources of inspiration and creativity that are more highly developed in you than in many people.

Your chart would suggest an involvement with music or harmony, for which you clearly have great potential. This is an aspect of yourself that you have learned to treasure, and it has been a great source of comfort to you on many occasions."

Cold readers who are fond of the Sherlock Strategy tend to build up a collection of favourite tell-tale clues. Quite how valuable these clues are is a matter of subjective assessment. What seems too 'obvious' (hence not worth mentioning) to one cold reader may seem quite delightfully subtle to another. Likewise, what one psychic considers to be a 'sure sign' may seem like a 'risky guess' to another.

With these caveats in mind, you may like to consider the eight examples below and see what conclusions you, as a psychic using the Sherlock Strategy, would come to. Please do not spend too long dwelling on these examples! I offer them only for fun. There are no 'definitive' answers and I would consider all of them either useless or unreliable for cold reading purposes. Nonetheless, you will find some possible answers at the back of the book in Appendix note 6.

'Sherlock Strategy' Guessing Game

1. A dark patch, like a faint bruise and roughly oval in shape, on the mid-to-left side of the client's throat about half-way down.

2. Female client. On the outer side of the left hand, in the area between the base of the thumb and the wrist, there appear to be several lines or streaks of faint red skin discolouration.

3. Female client. Several faint traces of a white, chalky powder around her lower leg and ankles, but *not* on her shoes.

4. Calluses on the right thumb, index and middle-finger.

5. Female client with a mole or visible birthmark of some kind on the face or neck.

6. Female client. It is noticed that she has with her a supply of mints and mint-flavoured chewing gum, which she seems to be using in an habitual manner.

7. Faint indications of blue powder, possibly chalk, around fingertips or cuffs.

8. Faint black or dark grey traces, like a smudge or greasy smear, seen on areas of the fingers or thumb, or near the side-pocket region of coat or jacket. (End of the Sherlock Strategy Guessing Game.)

Said rather than seen

The Sherlock Strategy can be applied to what is said as well as to what is seen. For example, suppose the psychic and the client enjoy a brief chat before the reading begins. The client, while taking off her coat and sitting down, may happen to say:

> "Sorry I'm late, the traffic was dreadful coming back from Woodvale."

'Woodvale' might mean nothing at all to the psychic. Alternatively, it might be an area of town associated with a major hospital, a golf club or a school with a good academic reputation. Perhaps it is known for its terrific gymnasium and health spa, or the Farmer's Market held twice a week, or a woodland area where people take their dogs for a walk. In each case, the psychic may ponder this clue and form some tentative guesses about the client's career, interests, family or current concerns.

The career from 26 years ago

Notwithstanding my earlier comments about deductive observation, there are certainly times when it pays dividends. I was once invited by Paramount Television to appear on the Leeza Gibbons TV show, which was taped in Los Angeles. The producers wanted me to demonstrate cold reading, so before the show I posed as a clairvoyant.

I sat in a small room off to one side of the TV studio. One at a time, four women from the studio audience (chosen at random by the production team) came in and sat down opposite me. I pretended to sense 'psychic impressions' that I scribbled down on a pad. Neither I nor any of the women exchanged a single word.

One of these women was in her mid-fifties. From her dress, hair and deportment, I felt that her self-presentation was a little bit better than most women know how to achieve. This suggested a background in fashion, beauty or modelling.

She wore quite a lot of silver and gold jewellery. It was all tasteful and well coordinated, but nonetheless a little ostentatious. This led me to think she might be the sort that enjoys attention, and knows how to 'dress to impress'. This led me to think she might have been involved in an area of show business.

Her posture (relaxed yet upright, the chin held level and not allowed to dip) suggested she knew about good breathing control. I guessed she knew about meditation, singing, or playing a wind instrument such as the flute. I concluded that at one time she might have been a singer or a musician. Since it tends to be singers who get the limelight, I decided to pursue that option.

What sort of singer? She seemed to lack the build, or the airs and graces, that one might associate with the classics. She struck me as being very dynamic, with plenty of energy and a good sense of fun. So, something lighter and more informal. Jazz? If so, her age suggested that her heyday would have coincided with the big band era, and the rise of popular jazz and 'swing'. I therefore concluded that she had probably been some sort of popular 'light jazz' cabaret or band singer.

I managed to talk to this particular woman later on, quite separately from the cold reading demonstration. I mentioned my 'impression' about her former singing career (suitably embellished in my usual cold reading style). It was very gratifying to discover that some 26 years previously she had been a professional cabaret artist and jazz singer!

She was astonished that I was able to describe what she had been doing 26 years previously, and considered this strong evidence of my 'psychic powers'. Even after the truth had been revealed (as it always was in my TV demonstrations), she suspected that I was genuinely clairvoyant.

Russian Doll

The Russian Doll consists of a statement that can have several possible layers of meaning. The psychic offers the initial statement and then, if necessary, explores other layers of meaning until she gets a hit. Russian Dolls are also known as 'Onion Skin' statements. Here is an example:

"Now I want to just say something to you about your daughter. You do have a daughter don't you?"

"No, I don't."

"Well, it could be that the person I'm trying to get to here is actually a daughter-in-law, is this making sense?"

"No, not really."

"Perhaps a god-daughter?"

"Well, there's my friend's little girl, I'm god-parent to her..."

"That's obviously the impression I was getting, I knew it was someone who was a daughter, or like a daughter, to you..."

In this hypothetical example, the psychic needed three bites at the cherry before she got the agreement she was looking for. On other occasions she might get an agreement at the first or second try. This element looks clumsy in print, but I have heard it used in real life without any objection at all from the client. Even if all variations on the theme get rejected there is always a way out (see 'The Win–Win Game' later).

'Music' and 'Collecting'

Here's another good Russian Doll:

"There's quite a clear indication here of music in your life."

If the client happens to play an instrument, the psychic wins and the client is impressed at the awesomely accurate psychic intuition. If not, the psychic modifies this initial statement until agreement is obtained. There are countless variations: you play a musical instrument / you once started learning to / you would like to / you sing / or would like to / you go to concerts and clubs / or you don't but you would like to do so more often / or at least you appreciate good live music / or you have a music collection that means a lot to you / or you listen to the radio a lot.

One more very successful Russian Doll concerns collecting. Any suitable phrasing will do, such as:

"I sense that you're a collector. Why is it I'm seeing a collection of some kind?"

In my experience, if the client is female and any age *except* in the middle of her wildest teenage years, then the 'collecting' Russian Doll stands an extremely good chance of yielding a hit. Many women collect things, from china dolls to potato chips 'resembling' famous people. However, the term 'collecting' can be interpreted in many different ways. If the client does not have a hobby or interest that involves collecting, she may agree that she is a 'collector' of friends, or experiences, or wisdom gleaned from life's ups and downs. In the curious realm of psychic readings, even risible twists of interpretation such as this can be the stuff of much-praised 'accuracy'.

The Mill

I once heard an excellent Russian Doll used by a spirit medium. Supposedly receiving messages from a dear departed loved one, the medium confidently announced that he (the person 'in spirit') had memories of 'the mill'. In England, where I live, there was a point during the twentieth century when the majority of the working population spent their days (or nights!) in a mill of some kind: cotton mill, steel mill, lead mill, flour mill and so on. Hence for clients of a certain age and background, this was a superb Russian Doll element that stood *every* chance of being a hit.

Progress Review

This concludes the third group of elements, which concerned extracting information from the client as surreptitiously as possible. Now we can move on to the final group of elements, which concern the client's future.

Elements about the future

Psychics are well-known for their ability to peer into the future on behalf of their clients. Few psychic readings would be complete without at least a little glimpse into tomorrow and beyond. This is a very important aspect of cold reading, and one that is so easy it is laughable (except to believers).

I have already clarified the fact that this book is about cold reading and not magic tricks. Let me stress this point one more time as I have often come across confusion on the issue.

Magical predictions

One of my friends in the magic world is an excellent and very stylish performer called John Lenehan. I remember seeing John when he was running a regular, weekly magic show at a theatre in north London. One of these shows took place a few days before the final of the Wimbledon Tennis Championship.

John wrote a prediction (sight unseen of the audience) and sealed it inside a padded envelope. He then asked a spectator in the audience to sign the envelope several times (there were no stooges involved). Next, John took a Polaroid photo of the spectator standing there in the theatre, holding the sealed envelope, and stapled this photo across the flap of the envelope. Finally, John gave the envelope to the spectator to take home and keep safe for one week.

The next show took place one week later, *after* the Wimbledon finals had taken place. The same woman brought along the envelope that had been in her possession all week. It was still covered in her own signatures and it still bore her own photo, just to prove that it was the exact same sealed envelope (which it really was). She was invited to join John on stage once more. She herself opened the envelope and took out the prediction that John had made the week before. It was a 100% accurate prediction of the results of the Wimbledon final!

The above is a factually accurate description of what happened. It may sound incredible, and it was, but there was nothing psychic or supernatural about it. It was a very ingenious piece of magical deception. (Those of my readers involved in the dark deceptive arts will recognise the ingenious effect once marketed by Lee Earle). John is an amazingly accomplished performer, not to mention extremely funny, but even he cannot *really* see into the future and accurately predict sports results!

Headlines and thoughts

Many magicians and mind readers have entertained their audiences by apparently predicting future events. I myself have had plenty of fun doing so over the years.

I once *posted* a sealed prediction to what was, at the time, Britain's most popular daytime TV show ('This Morning' with Richard Madeley and Judy Finnegan). I sent the sealed prediction to the show two days before I was due to appear on it. The envelope was signed on air by the show's presenters and then locked away in a safe by the producer.

Two days later, when I appeared on the show, presenter Richard Madeley first of all confirmed that the envelope had been locked away and that I had not been allowed anywhere near it. He himself then opened the envelope live on air, without me even so much as touching it. It contained an exact prediction of that morning's newspaper headlines!

On another occasion, I appeared on a discussion show hosted by Esther Rantzen, one of the most successful and respected figures in British television. Before the studio audience arrived, the TV people shot some video of me writing a prediction, although the camera angle meant no-one could see exactly what I wrote. I sealed my prediction in an envelope and handed it to Esther Rantzen, who signed it and kept it. This video was proof that the prediction was written and sealed before the show even began.

Later, the studio audience arrived and the show got under way. One of the other guests was respected scientist and writer Susan Blackmore. She was invited to choose a member of the audience at random. I had no influence whatsoever over Susan's choice and I had no idea who she would choose. The member of the audience selected by Susan happened to be a woman called Sam (I presume short for 'Samantha').

Sam was invited to stand up and just *think* of any set of initials. All this time, host Esther Rantzen was holding the sealed package containing my prediction. I was standing on the far side of the studio, nowhere near Esther, Sam or the sealed prediction package.

Sam announced the initials she was thinking of: T and H. Esther Rantzen handed the sealed prediction package over to Sam. Sam opened it, and inside was a pad of paper on which I had earlier written the initials 'T H' in large, bold letters.

The tricks trade

Some of these demonstrations are so baffling that some people feel believe they must involve at least *some* genuine psychic ability. On a few occasions, people have accused me of possessing at least a trace of genuine psychic ability but choosing to lie about it (although it's hard to see why I would do so). Many of my friends in the worlds of magic and mind-reading have similar tales to tell. One of my friends even had people campaigning to ban her performance on the basis that she was a witch and her show involved black magic.

Without wishing to spoil the fun, let me give you a cast-iron assurance that these demonstrations are magic tricks. Intriguing, ingenious and hopefully entertaining tricks — but tricks nonetheless. They do not involve psychic powers of any kind.

How are these tricks done? If your interest is casual, I do not want to spoil the fun by telling you. If your interest is sincere, take up magic as a hobby and eventually you will find out. It could take a while, though.

Enough of magic tricks, and back to cold reading. Here are several ways to predict future events within the context of a psychic reading.

Peter Pan Predictions

Peter Pan predictions simply involves predicting whatever the client wants to hear. This may seem such a simplistic ruse as not to be worth mentioning. On the other hand, it is such a key aspect of the psychic seduction that it would be incongruous not to include it in this section. Indeed, some sources would say this is the single most important element of all.

Of course, Peter Pan predictions are found in many places besides psychic readings. Every sales message or advertisement promises the same thing: the purchaser's future will be better for having made the purchase than it would be otherwise. This is untrue at least as often as it is true, but we tend to carry on believing it regardless.

In the context of a psychic reading, Peter Pan predictions are usually reserved for whichever of the Main Themes the client seems most interested in. Health worries? Not to worry, an eventual return to good health is indicated. Financial problems? They will all be sorted out in the long run. The new romance? Congratulations, it is going to be a success!

It is as simple as that. Whatever the client most desires to come true, the psychic makes sure she sees it happening. In this day and age, this kind of highly reassuring message is perhaps the only one people cannot readily obtain from the media or anywhere else. It seems many people are prepared to pay good money to hear it said in a way that at least *sounds* sincere, reassuring and credible.

Of course, any statement about the future is perfectly safe from the psychic's point of view. At the time of the reading, the client cannot check the statement one way or the other. Afterwards, the predictions that come true will be remembered and cited as evidence of the psychic's awesome gift. The ones that do not will be forgotten.

Pollyanna Pearls

These are fairly bland predictions that follow a set formula. They focus on one area of the client's life, and say that things that may have been difficult lately will improve soon. They are named after Pollyanna, the irrepressibly optimistic heroine of Eleanor Porter's 1913 novel. A typical example might go like this:

"Financially, it's been a bit of a bumpy ride these past couple of years, but the next 18 month or so will be a lot easier."

Psychics can apply Pollyanna Pearls to most facets of life, and to almost any type of reading. Here are some other examples that illustrate possible themes and variations.

The tarot reader:

"The spread of the cards suggests relationships have been a source of concern over the past 14 months, perhaps not in ways that even your close friends would fully understand. However, these concerns are due to fade, and the next 6 to 12 months offer happier and smoother prospects."

The spiritualist:

"I have your late grandfather here with me now. He's telling you not to worry so much about the house and about money. He knows you've had your worries in recent times, but he wants to let you know that financially there's a much better spell ahead, and that your plans will go well."

The astrologer:

"There have been elements of conflict in your chart over the past 6 to 12 months and these could have led to career difficulties. However, Saturn has recently entered your chart. This indicates some beneficial changes that will see you on a much more fulfilled path before the end of the year."

The Pollyanna Pearl is a highly versatile element and can hardly go wrong since it is non-verifiable (at the time of the reading). In any case, everyone likes to hear glad tidings.

Certain Predictions

These are sure-fire, blue-chip, gold-plated predictions that cannot fail. Here are some examples:

"Someone new is going to come into your life."

"A minor illness or injury is indicated."

"You will experience problems with an investment, or with something you have bought."

Did you spot the trick involved? The psychic conveniently forgot to say *when* these things will happen. Since the psychic has not mentioned any time scale, it is impossible for her to be wrong.

If these events happen quite soon, the psychic takes the credit for her highly accurate 'instant' predictions. If they happen years and years later, the psychic takes the credit for having seen a long way into the future. If they never happen at all before the client passes away, she is by then in no position to ask for a refund.

I once saw a documentary in which several psychics were secretly filmed while they gave readings. Some of these readings included predictions about the future. The production team went back to the same psychics six months later, and showed them that their predictions had not come true. The psychics said the predictions would come true in time. The production team patiently waited yet another six months, and then went back to show that the predictions had *still* not come to pass. Of course they got exactly the same answer.

Borgs

A friend of mine was once giving a reading. The client had scribbled on a piece of paper the one thing that was on her mind. All she had written was, "borg". It took my friend a moment to realise what this meant. As he correctly guessed, the client's daughter was due to have a baby and she (the client) was curious as to whether it would be a boy or a girl.

Borgs are predictions about events that can only go one of two ways. Will the client get the promotion she wants or not? Will company X's stock be higher or lower one month from now? Will the red team or the blue team win the championship?

Psychics tend to latch on to these questions and offer confident predictions as to the outcome. With the odds immutably fixed at 50/50, the more predictions the psychic makes the more hits she is bound to get. If she makes a hundred such predictions in a year, by the end of the year she will have about 50 totally accurate predictions to her credit. She can carefully document *all* her predictions so that later, if any turn out correct, she can present proof of what she said and when she said it. These documented predictions come in handy for positive PR and sceptic-bashing.

What about the predictions that fail? It is unlikely anyone will document the psychic's predictions and then get the chance to question her about the failures. In the unlikely event of a psychic being confronted in this way, she has several escape hatches. She may claim she was mis-quoted, or only selectively quoted. Alternatively, she may say that a particular *report* of her prediction was inaccurate, but the prediction itself was correct. The most disarming defence is just to smile sweetly, admit the error and point out that it doesn't matter:

"Yes, I do get one or two predictions wrong. It's a process of interpretation and sometimes that interpretation can be very difficult. I have never claimed to be infallible, have I? But I know I'm right far more often than not."

Here's the slightly more defensive version:

"I'm not asking anyone to believe anything. Yes, I make mistakes. But my clients know the value of the services I provide, and frankly they are the people that matter."

Likely Predictions

For these predictions, the psychic makes a guess about the future that stands a reasonable chance of being correct. Unlike the 'Certain Predictions', listed above, these *do* include a time scale. For example:

"Within the next month, you will receive an unexpected contact from someone you haven't heard from in quite a while."

"Within the next week or two, you will hear of a legal matter that could directly affect you."

Both these predictions are quite likely to come true, since things like this happen all the time. Nonetheless, by the strange and self-serving rules of the psychic industry, such predictions are apparently the very stuff of wonder. Here is another:

"In the year ahead I foresee an accident involving you, or a member of your family, and broken or falling glass."

Again, this stands a fair chance of coming true since it happens all the time. You should also bear in mind the tremendous latitude that is applied to psychic pronouncements. The 'glass' mentioned above could be almost anything: a wineglass, a window, a mirror, a car headlight, a bottle, a pair of spectacles, a glass table, a fish tank, a skylight and so on. It could even be something that merely *resembles* glass, such as the ice-covered surface of a pond.

Unlikely Predictions

Surprisingly enough, as well as the Likely Predictions mentioned above, the psychic may also find it worthwhile to deliberately make an Unlikely Prediction once in a while. If it fails, there is no harm done. On the other hand, if by some outrageous fluke it happens to come true, it affords ample opportunities for glowing PR and strengthens the faith of the devoted. It also makes a very useful stick with which to beat sceptics. For all these reasons, the psychic may, just once in a while, offer a forecast that she knows is unlikely to come true:

> "Four weeks from now, you will meet someone with exactly the same initials as yourself."

> "You will see an old friend driving a car of silver colours, with a dog in the rear seat."

By their very nature, most Unlikely Predictions will fail. However, the one or two that *are* successful can be put forward as especially persuasive proof of the psychic's powers. After all, the more unlikely the event predicted, the more amazing the prediction is deemed to be.

If the psychic gives just one reading a day, and incorporates just one Unlikely Prediction per reading, she may well get one or two hits by the end of the year. While this may not be many, these kinds of predictions have tremendous PR value simply by being so self-evidently unlikely. By such means are great reputations founded.

Fact Pacts

These are straightforward, factual predictions about the medium-term future. For instance:

> "You will be involved in a holiday, or a long journey, next March."

> "In June, you will hear news of an unexpected celebration."

> "Before the end of the year, I see you finding a valuable family memento that you thought you had lost for good."

There is little or no artifice involved in such predictions. The psychic simply takes a guess that may or may not come true. Nonetheless, the predictions are likely to work in her favour.

The first reason is that clients remember the predictions that come true and forget the rest. Secondly, only the clients whose predictions come true tend to talk about them. It makes for highly intriguing conversation to tell your friends about a prediction that turned out to be right. Few people ever think it worth mentioning that they went to see a psychic, she made a prediction and it turned out to be incorrect.

Another factor in the psychic's favour is that clients are prone to invest readings with the benefit of hindsight. Suppose the psychic merely predicted, 'an important journey sometime next year, maybe around March or April'. Suppose, too, that the client happens to get sent on a long business trip around June. When she tells the story she may well quote the psychic as having said 'You will go on a business trip overseas in the middle of next year, June or July'. The psychic's actual words were quite different and off the mark. But who cares about that?

Self-fulfilling Predictions

Another neat trick is for the psychic to make predictions that possess the virtue of being self-fulfilling. These generally pertain to aspects of the client's mood and personality. For example:

> "You will begin to adopt a more positive and friendly outlook. You will let go of many old grievances, and start being a good friend to yourself and to others. You will soon have a larger social circle than at present."

This kind of prediction is likely to be self-fulfilling in many cases. If the client goes away convinced that she is about to become more popular, she may well feel very happy at the prospect. Since she is happier, she is more pleasant and sociable. Since she is more sociable, she makes friends more easily. Another successful psychic peek through the curtain of time!

There are any number of possible variations: gaining new confidence, resolving a relationship issue, becoming less anxious, tackling a problem with renewed determination and so on. In each case, just believing the psychic's words may be enough for the prediction to come true.

Foggy Forecasts

I have already stated the inadequacy of the 'vagueness' theory of cold reading (see 'Popular Misconceptions'). However, it is true that for any psychic in the prediction business, vagueness is a valuable asset. The point of wrapping a prophecy in dense layers of fog is not that *nothing* can be seen in the mist, but that *anything* can be seen in it. Many psychic predictions practically elevate vagueness to an art form. I refer to such typical gems as:

> "A journey is indicated."

> "I see a new source of fulfilment in your life."

> "Your life will enter a new phase of progress."

> "A surprising aspect to the month of June will have significant implications that only become clear much later in the year."

Astrological readings are particularly well-suited to this markedly fatuous kind of prediction. This may be because its followers are, by definition, capable of seeing significance where none exists.

Unverifiable Predictions

Another ruse employed by psychics is to make predictions that the client can never verify either way. Here is an example:

> "Someone you know will secretly harbour a grudge against you. They will plan to put obstacles in your way, but you will overcome their plans without even realising it."

Take a moment to study the careful wording used here. You will see that the client cannot possibly know if this prediction ever comes true or not. Here is another:

> "At the place where you work, there will be some behind-the-scenes dealings that do not involve you, but that will be to your advantage in the long term."

The psychic who makes Unverifiable Predictions can never be wrong. And a psychic who is never wrong is a happy psychic.

One-way Verifiable Predictions

One-way Verifiable Predictions are perhaps the single neatest form of prediction in cold reading. These predictions *can be* verified, but *only* if they come true. If they do not come true, this failure can *never* be proved. Here is an example:

> "A friend will be inclined to telephone you with news that has an effect on your career, but may decide at the last minute not to do so."

Let us look at the possibilities. If some friend or other does call as described, purely by coincidence, then the prediction is a hit. If they do not, this can be attributed to the fact that they decided not to, which the psychic mentioned as a possibility. Here is another example:

> "Someone you have had a professional connection with in the past may decide to get in touch with news of an interesting career opportunity. However, they may realise they can't really offer you what you're worth, and decide against it."

As before, the psychic can only be proved right but can never be proved wrong. To anyone in the psychic trade, One-way Verifiable Predictions are a thing of beauty, and the ability to churn them out more or less at will is a skill worth cultivating.

Public Prophecies

The techniques listed so far pertain chiefly to predictions made in the context of a private reading. However, many psychics like to try their hand at the occasional public pronouncement. It is therefore worth mentioning some of the methods used by psychics to build a reputation for high-profile media-friendly public prophecy. I do not regard these as part of cold reading as such, but I have included them here for completeness.

Psychics sometimes get asked about public events, such as the outcome of a sports contest or a political election. The psychic can either go with the current betting or deliberately go against it. If she takes the first option, she has a good chance of being right although this won't look very impressive. If she takes the second option, she stands less chance of being right but will appear all the more impressive if she gets lucky. Either option has its advantages, and neither poses any danger to the psychic's reputation. If she gets a prediction wrong, so what? In most cases, no-one cares, no-one remembers.

In extremely rare cases, some unusually assiduous investigator may take the trouble to document a psychic's incorrect prediction, to get all the facts correct, and to confront the psychic with this failure. If this happens, the psychic can simply serve up a good-natured reply about human striving and imperfection:

> "I never said I'm infallible, and of course I can be wrong. We're all on a path of learning, and I'm still learning my craft even after all these years. Sometimes I stumble, I fail. But I'm just trying to do the best I can with the gift I've been given, and on the whole I think my track record is pretty good."

Golden disasters

Some psychics get involved in the disaster business, and care to predict earthquakes, airplane crashes, assassinations and similar tragic news. The rule here is for the psychic to predict vague, predict often and document everything. Then she can scream from the rooftops if she happens to get one right (which has to happen eventually, persistence being the virtue that it is).

Red and blue

Another time-honoured method is to make conflicting predictions in different places. In magazine A, the psychic predicts the red team will win. In magazine B, she predicts the blue team will win.

After the event, guess which cutting gets pasted into the scrapbook and added to future press releases? It is very unlikely that anyone is going to dig up the truth about these conflicting guesses. Even if they do, the psychic can always claim she changed her mind, or the 'vibrations' she works from changed after she made the first prediction. There is always an excuse!

Having briefly discussed public predictions, I can now share the most effective, most powerful prediction technique I have *ever* come across: the Neverwas Prediction.

Bonus: The Neverwas Prediction

This is not a cold reading element as such, so I have not counted it in the total of 38 elements that I said I would include in this book. However, it is so wonderful that I thought I would mention it before concluding this section.

The Neverwas Prediction is only relevant to press interviews and similar public situations. Assume that the psychic is going to be interviewed by a journalist. Before the interview, the psychic *makes up* a story about some amazing prediction she made a while ago that came true. The fact that this never actually happened is irrelevant. All that matters is that it's a good story the journalist can use. If it involves a twist ending, all the better.

The interview takes place, and the psychic mentions this amazing prediction (that never actually happened). Let us see what might happen once the interview is over.

Neverwas: first scenario

The journalist who writes up the interview *may* bother to add a disclaimer to the prediction story, such as, "Psychic X *claims* that five years ago...". This makes it clear that the prediction is merely a claim, not a verified fact. However, not all journalists would regard such a disclaimer as either necessary or desirable. Hence the prediction story might get written up as if it were documented fact. Once the story is part of the news archives, it can get repeated and recycled forever.

Neverwas: second scenario

Suppose the conscientious journalist *does* include the disclaimer. The psychic is still in with a chance. Before the interview gets printed, the disclaimer could get left out for any number of reasons, such as an over-worked sub-editor hastily shortening the interview to fit the page. The disclaimer gets deleted and the fictional prediction story once again gets printed as if it were fact.

Neverwas third scenario

Suppose the story duly appears in print, with the disclaimer intact. Some time later, another journalist may be preparing a piece about the same psychic. This second journalist checks out the news archives, sees the prediction story and decides to include it in his article. The story gets rehashed in a slightly 'tidied up' form, *without* the dull disclaimer. Yet again the story ends up enshrined as fact in the press archives, to be mentioned whenever the psychic so desires.

In all these different ways, the Neverwas Prediction can become set in stone as a piece of factual news archive. It may go on to appear in magazine articles or books for decades afterwards. A documentary film-maker may even decide to arrange a 'reconstruction' of the whole story, perhaps failing to acknowledge to the viewing millions the distinction between 'reconstruction' and 'made up rubbish'.

Far be it from me to suggest whether this technique has ever been used in real life. It is mentioned here only as a possibility.

Progress Review

This concludes the fourth and final group of elements concerning predictions. It also concludes the section concerning the elements of the reading. Now it is time to see what happens when things go slightly wrong for the psychic.

How CR Works 4/7: The Win–Win Game

So far we have looked at the Set Up, the Main Themes, and the Elements involved in the cold reading process.

It should be clear that these elements *can* deliver wonderful hits, and are likely to do so in many cases. However, there are going to be times when the psychic offers a statement that the client rejects. Now and again the client will say that a statement is incorrect or just doesn't mean anything to her.

This isn't a problem for the psychic. There are many ways in which she can still be right, or at the very least *partially* right. This is part of the joy of psychic readings: if the client accepts a statement then the psychic wins and if she rejects a statement the psychic wins anyway!

There are two main ways for psychics to deal with a negative response: revisions and codas. I will deal with the revisions first, because I think they are more interesting and useful. Later we will look at the two commonest codas.

There are numerous revisions that a psychic might use, but in this section I am just going to mention the eight that I think are most useful and versatile.

Focus

This revision applies when at least *part* of a statement is right, even if it's just one word or one idea. The psychic places all the focus and attention on the part of the statement that is right and allows the rest to fade away, forgotten and unmentioned:

> "I'm sensing the name Jane or Jenna in connection with your place of work. Someone you don't necessarily know very well but you see her often. Can you place this person?"

If the client happens to work with anyone called Jane or Jenna, or anyone with a name that sounds similar, this is a hit. However, suppose the client says:

> *"No, not really. I know a Joanne, but she's nothing to do with work. She's a friend from my school days."*

> "Yes, that must be who I was getting. I was sensing a female name starting with J, you know, Jane or Joanne or something like that, and I knew it had to be someone you have known for quite a long time. And you *have* known her a long time, haven't you?"

The psychic places all the focus and emphasis on the bits that are right, and simply forgets about the rest.

A slight refinement is for the psychic to hint that she only got something wrong because she did not trust her psychic powers:

> "Oh, she's called Joanne is she? Well that'll teach me! I *wanted* to say Joanne but then I got this impression about Jane or that kind of sound. I should learn to trust my first instincts, shouldn't I? Okay, but nonetheless I knew that there was someone in your life with this name that you've known a long time. That's right isn't it?"

When using the Focus revision, the psychic's delivery and tone of voice can help to make the error seem a trivial distraction of no consequence. Example:

> "And this house you lived in at the time, I see a number 2 on the door. That's right isn't it?"

If yes, this is a hit. If not, the psychic says:

> "Well, all right, I'm obviously confused about the *exact* number but not to worry, it doesn't matter. This *house* that I'm seeing is the important thing, and the reason I want to mention this house is that..."

The psychic goes on to talk about something completely different, forgetting about the problematic numeral as if it had never been mentioned. The client can generally be relied upon to also forget about it. A happy conspiracy of forgetfulness adds greatly to the impressive nature of many psychic readings.

Awareness

The psychic suggests that her statement is correct, but the client may not realise this as she isn't *aware* of all the facts:

> "I'm sensing the name Jane or Jenna in connection with your place of work. Someone you don't necessarily know very well but you see her often. Can you place this person?"

> *"Not really, no, I don't think I know anyone with either of those names."*

> "Actually, there's a good chance this might not be your place of work. It might be someone your husband or a friend of yours works with, at some office or something like that, and you might not know them personally."

The psychic is basically saying she is right, but the client isn't in a position to know that she is right. A useful variation is to suggest that *nobody* is aware of the crucial information:

> "Actually, this might be someone whose first name is actually Jane, but she always uses her middle name for some reason. Even people who have known her for a very long time aren't aware that in fact she regularly uses her middle name, which I sense is quite different."

Another variation is to suggest that there's a reason why a given piece of information might not be available to the client, such as embarrassment:

> "I'm sensing this name Jane or Jenna, and she's recently had a medical issue to deal with, yes?"

If yes, this is a hit. If not, the psychic says:

> "Actually, she may have kept rather quiet about it. I sense it's perhaps not something she would talk about much. I don't think it was anything particularly serious so we don't need to dwell on it."

Yet another variation is the suggest that the client's memory may be at fault, or that she was never fully aware of the situation in the first place. This can be made to sound entirely forgivable:

> "And when you were younger, I see an accident involving water. Does this make sense to you?"

If yes, this is a hit. If not, the psychic says:

> "I sense it's going back some time, perhaps when you were very young. You may not remember much about it now."

The Awareness revision is never used in such a way as to make the client feel stupid or ignorant. The psychic always makes it clear that the lack of awareness is entirely understandable and blameless.

Subjectivity

This revision applies to statements that involve opinion, judgment or assessment. The psychic suggests that her statement is correct if you allow for the fact that some things are subjective or relative.

> "I sense that this person, Joanne, has been quite successful with her career and in particular with money. This seems to be a very positive area for her."

> *"I don't think I'd say that, not really. She doesn't have a very good job, and she was out of work for a while and I think she had some financial difficulties."*

"Well, that's fine, but you know success can mean different things to different people. Although she may have had some hard times, she didn't let things get her down. She picked herself up, stayed positive and got on with her life. In the tarot, wealth is more about personal qualities than money in the bank and that's what I meant by success: being a fighter, showing strength of character."

It is important to note that this revision is only ever used to go from negative judgments to positive ones, and never the other way around. Consider this example.

"You have had some success in relationships and you are a good and loving partner."

"Not really. To be honest, I haven't had a lot of success in that department."

"Well, okay, maybe you haven't met the love of your life, but that's not what I mean. When I say 'success', you're the sort of person who has always been honest in relationships and been true to your values. You have always done your best to treat people well. That's the success I'm referring to, and in the fullness of time I can tell you that your honesty and your principles will lead to great success in relationships."

In this example, the client feels she has *not* been very successful in relationships but the psychic uses the Subjectivity revision to help her see things a different way. The negative feeling is transformed into a positive one. The psychic would never use this revision to turn a positive feeling into a negative one!

The Subjectivity revision is more useful and versatile than may be obvious at first glance. Clearly, it can be used whenever the psychic has expressed a judgment or an opinion. We all know that terms such as 'good', 'successful' and 'positive' can mean different things to different people depending on their point of view. However, the Subjectivity revision can also sometimes be applied to statements that seems more factual and definitive:

"And your sister is older than you, isn't she?"

"No, she's quite a bit younger."

"Ah yes, I see, I was actually picking up an impression from *her* point of view, not yours. It's clearer now."

Here is another example:

"The cards suggest that your current job is one you have only been doing for a short time."

"No, I've been working there for years actually."

"Yes, you've been there a long time, I understand that, but I'm getting the sense that there are some people there, at your place of work, who have only joined relatively recently. *They* have only known you there for a short time. That's what I was getting at."

In the psychic realm, almost everything is subjective or relative.

Time

The psychic suggests that her statement, if it is not correct *now*, either was correct or will be in the future. Here is a simple example:

"I'm sensing the name Jane or Jenna in connection with your place of work. Can you place this person?"

"No, I don't think so."

"That's fine. I sense that someone with that sort of name has been significant at some point in the past. It's okay if you don't remember. We all meet a lot of people on our journey through life and we can't remember everybody."

If the psychic chooses to refer to the past, as in this example, it is *theoretically* possible that the client could still reject the statement. The client could steadfastly maintain that no-one with a name like 'Jane' has ever been significant in her life. I have never seen this happen, and it's highly unlikely that it ever would in a real-life reading. Nonetheless, some cold readers prefer to play safe and always refer to the future rather than the past:

"Well, someone with that name will be significant soon, maybe in the next few weeks. Will you look out for that?"

The Time revision is more versatile than you might think. In its commonest and easiest form, the psychic shifts from the present tense to the past or future tense. However, the psychic can always mention that time is a rather fluid concept in the psychic world. This opens up more possibilities. For example, a statement about the future, if incorrect, can be twisted into the correct shape:

"I also foresee that you, or someone close to you, will be moving house in the near future."

"That's sort of right, but it's not in the future. We actually just finished moving house about a month ago."

"That's absolutely fine. I could see you moving house and, for some reason, I thought it was coming up in the near future. Of course the past is the source of the future, and the future bears the imprint of the past, so you see time is rather a fluid concept in the psychic world..."

Metaphor

The psychic suggests that her statement, while it may be wrong in terms of plain, literal fact, is correct when understood in some non-literal way. In other words, the statement has to be understood in a metaphorical, figurative, allegorical or poetic way. A more general form of the Metaphor revision is for the psychic to suggest that she was working on the level of feelings and emotions rather than facts.

Here is an example I remember from a reading given many years ago by an entertainer in the same field as myself. At the time, he was giving demonstrating his psychic prowess for a female journalist who had been born and raised in Ireland, and who happened to have short hair. At one point in the reading, he offered this statement:

"You used to have your hair long when you were younger, didn't you?"

"No, I've always worn it short, actually. Where I grew up we weren't allowed to have long hair."

My friend, thinking quickly, correctly guessed that if a young girl is strictly forbidden to wear her hair long she will probably develop a strong desire to do so. He therefore offered this follow-up statement:

"Yes, I know, but what I mean is you *wanted* to wear it long, didn't you?"

The client agreed that this has been the case, and this particular statement was accepted as a hit! Moreover, it was taken as evidence that the wonderful 'psychic vibrations' reveal our inner selves and deep desires, not just outward appearances. The statement was wrong in fact, but right when understood in terms of feelings and emotions.

Here's another example.

"There are indications here of new education. It could be that you have been studying recently, maybe to do with professional exams or taking classes of some kind."

If yes, this is a hit. If the client says no, she isn't studying or doing anything of that nature, the psychic says:

"Well, you know, this isn't necessarily to do with classrooms and textbooks, that's not really the picture I'm getting. I meant education in the broader sense. After all, experience is the finest teacher of them all, isn't it? I just feel that one or two recent experiences have maybe taught you a thing or two, even if it's only learning new things about yourself or about life and how people tick, you know what I mean?"

Here is another example:

"The cards indicate a period of travel, perhaps you're planning a trip abroad or you may have just returned from one."

If yes, this is a hit. If the client says no, she has neither been travelling nor intends to, the psychic says:

"Well of course this doesn't have to be about suitcases and passports. There are many kinds of travelling and many kinds of journeys, and in a sense life is the greatest journey of them all isn't it? The cards could be suggesting that recent events have been like a journey for you, perhaps a journey of discovery or of understanding. Maybe recent events have given you a new outlook on things or given you reason to re-think a thing or two."

The Metaphor revision boils down to the fact that if you give yourself enough poetic licence, almost anything can be understood to refer to almost anything else.

The Metaphor revision is very similar to the Interpretation revision, which we will meet later. The only real difference is that the Metaphor revision is quite broad and usually applies to a complete statement or idea, whereas the Interpretation revision is quite specific and usually applies to a single word.

Applicability

The psychic suggests that her statement is correct, but may apply to someone other than the client. This may sound rather clumsy, but it is actually a very effective revision. Here's an example:

> "The spread of the cards indicate that you have recently had some significant financial news, or perhaps a financial matter is weighing on your mind."

If yes, this is a hit. If not, the psychic says:

> "It's quite a clear impression, although it could apply to someone you know or someone in your immediate circle. You have definitely been near someone with an important financial matter on their mind."

If the client thinks about this for a moment and can recall such a conversation, this creates the impression that the psychic's awesome powers can reach as far as the client's family, friends and social circle. Very impressive!

If the client cannot recall any such discussion, the psychic still wins by suggesting that the client may not be aware of all the relevant facts (this is the Awareness revision we saw earlier).

One more example:

> "There are signs here of new romance, or at least of romantic feelings that the cards suggest could develop in a very positive way for you."

> *"No, I don't know what that could be. Actually,. I'm perfectly happy with the relationship I'm in and there's no-one new in my life."*

> "That's fine, and I see that your own journey along the path of romance is settled and you've made a good match. But there's someone close to you, perhaps a good friend or someone you see from time to time, who has recently had some new developments in her romantic life, and I expect she'll want to talk to you about it soon. Will you look out for that?"

This is the Applicability revision blended with the Time revision that we have already looked at.

Measurement

This revision applies to statements that involve measurement of time, distance, age or anything else. The psychic suggests that her statement is correct provided we measure things in the right way or adopt the right criteria. Here's a simple example:

"And this Joanne person is older than you, isn't she?"

"No, she's quite a bit younger."

"That's fine. She may be younger in terms of actual years, but there are many ways of thinking about age. I sense she has a maturity about her that could lead some people to think she's the same age as you or even older. Or maybe her tastes or interests are ones you would normally associate with an older person. That's what I'm getting at."

Here's another example:

"And this person who is linked with you romantically is someone you've known for quite a long time."

"Not really, we met quite recently. It's all happened rather quickly."

"That's fine. When I say 'quite some time' all I'm getting at is that you didn't meet yesterday or this afternoon, right? You've had time to get to know one another. And while you say it's only been a few weeks, in one sense you've been waiting a long time to meet this person, haven't you? That's what I was getting at."

This revision hinges on the fact that measurements can be relative rather than absolute. Is three weeks a long time? Compared to ten years, no; compared to ten minutes, yes. Is fifty kilometres a long distance? Yes if you compare it to a shorter distance, no if you compare it to a much longer one. While this may not be a particularly sophisticated revision, it comes in very handy in many psychic readings.

(On the subject of relativism, an American friend once said the difference between Americans and British people is that Americans think a hundred years is a long time while British people think a hundred miles is a long way to drive.)

Interpretation

The psychic suggests that her statement is correct provided a particular word or phrase is interpreted correctly. For example, if the psychic is giving a tarot reading, she may hazard a guess that the client has a sister:

"I see a financial transaction involving your sister."

If the client rejects this on the basis that she does not *have* a sister, the psychic immediately responds with something like this:

"That's fine. Within tarot, we often use 'sister' to mean any female with whom you have a close friendship or whom you know well..."

Broadening and adapting the meaning in this way provides a much greater chance of obtaining a hit or a near-hit. Similarly, the astrologer may offer something like this:

> "If I go back to last September, the influence of Pluto in your fifth house at this time would suggest you benefited financially, or came into some money."

If the client rejects this, the astrologer can smoothly introduce this kind of revision:

> "Well, I said 'money', but in astrological terms we rarely think of wealth as purely coins and hard cash. What I really meant was wealth in terms of your life and fulfilment."

Provided the client can think of any bit of good news during the period referred to, the psychic can count this as another hit.

Spiritualists are especially fond of this revision. Since they alone can tell us how dead people think and feel, they can invoke whatever explanations seem expedient at the time. A common example arises when the psychic has mis-stated the client's relationship to the person coming through from the spirit world:

> "And I have an elderly gentleman with me now who says you may well have been trying to communicate with him, since he passed recently. I sense this could be your father."

At this point the client might point out that her father is alive, but that her brother passed recently. The psychic might then ask a Direct Question to establish that the client's brother was older than her, and say:

> "Oh, I understand now. What he meant was that when you were both young, there were often times when he was left with responsibility for you, and he was almost like a father figure to his little sister."

This would be another triumph for the special semantic licence granted to psychics. There are always themes and variations available to the skilled cold reader. In the example above, it really does not matter whether or not the brother's age turns out to be convenient. Even if he had been much, much younger, the psychic could offer a line like this:

> "Oh, it's coming through more clearly now. It was me that was confused, not your brother! I got the word 'father' and I jumped the gun. He was trying to explain to me not that he *was* your father, but that you and he both had the *same* father... that's right, isn't it?"

There is always a way out!

The Interpretation revision is very closely related to the Metaphor revision, in that both involve a shift from a literal to a non-literal meaning. It would be possible to list them under one heading, but I prefer to list them separately.

Notes on the revisions

Having listed eight common revisions, I just want to add a few brief notes about them.

First of all, this list of revisions is not exhaustive. There are many other ways in which a seemingly 'wrong' statement can be twisted into sounding correct or near enough. However, these eight are among the most useful to know about.

Secondly, these revisions do not have to be used separately and individually. It is quite common to blend them together. I jave already given an example that combined the Applicability and Time revisions. Combining different revisions gives the psychic even more ways to be right.

Thirdly, these eight revisions are not defined in strict and mutually exclusive terms. They are only loosely defined and they do overlap to some extent. Also, some of the examples I've provided in this section could have been placed under two or more different revisions. In the wonderful realm of psychic revelation, all that matters is that the psychic always wins.

Two codas

We have looked at eight different revisions and how they enable the psychic to be right even if she is wrong. There are two additional techniques for overcoming disagreement and negative responses. I refer to these as codas, since in essence they are ways of drawing one part of a reading to a close.

The first coda is called 'Persist and leave hanging'. This is a very reliable coda that can kill off more or less any negative response. It involves three phases:

(a) the psychic persists with the statement and tries to win at least partial agreement

(b) she acts puzzled, and invites the client to share responsibility for the 'discrepancy'

(c) she leaves the discrepancy unresolved, in case the client finds a match later on

A typical example might start like this:

"I'm getting the name Jane, why is that significant to you?"

"I can't think. No. No-one I know."

A negative response! First of all, the psychic persists with the original statement. Given a bit more time and encouragement, the client might well come up with a link. Another reason for persisting with the original statement is that most people are reluctant to say they are 100% *definite* and *certain* about something, especially if the psychic puts them on the spot. They may well come up with some sort of link just to save feeling uncomfortable. It might go something like this:

"You're quite sure?"

"Pretty sure. I don't think I know anyone by that name."

"You're *absolutely positive* about that?"

"Well, I can't think of anyone. No, not really."

"You're *certain* that you know absolutely *nobody* with that name and you *never* have done?"

This may sound rather aggressive, but the psychic's manner and personality can make it seem quite acceptable. I have heard more than one radio psychic (under some pressure to deliver 'instant' results) use this kind of approach.

Very few clients will stick to their guns under this kind of questioning. However, if they do, the psychic simply moves on to the next phase: acting puzzled and inviting the client to share her bewilderment. Incidentally, some psychics will also mention that they do *not* want the client to try and make the statement fit. This comes across as endearingly honest:

"Well, all right, I don't understand it any more than you do. I'm getting this impression of the name Jane and whether it means anything to you or not all I can do is tell you what I see. I'm not asking you to try and make it fit, that's not the point. To be honest, I'm not often wrong so will you carry on thinking about that? Because I feel sure there is a link but obviously you can't think of it at the moment..."

If the client does eventually remember someone called 'Jane', the psychic gets extra points for the depth of her insight. If no such triumph emerges, the point simply gets forgotten and the psychic never mentions it again. What matters is that this part of the reading has been brought to an end, and the psychic can happily move on to talk about something else.

The second coda involves the gracious acceptance of defeat. This is the last refuge! If all else fails, the psychic can at least say something like this:

> "Well, when I'm wrong I'm wrong and I'm not too proud to admit it.
> I wish I could always be a 100% right, but then don't we all?
> Anyway, let me move on to the next area I want to look at with you,
> which is travel..."

In this way the psychic cuts her losses and moves on. She leaves the problem behind, where it will be quietly forgotten, and at the same time she comes across as endearingly honest.

Progress Review

We have looked at The Set Up, Main Themes and Elements. We have also seen how the psychic gets out of awkward errors using Win–Win techniques. Next, we will look at presentational aspects of the reading.

How CR Works 5/7: Presentation

There is more to cold reading than getting the actual content right. Several aspects of presentation can also greatly assist the success of a reading. This section looks at some of the more important ones.

Cultivating feedback

In theory, a psychic reading could consist of the psychic doing all the talking and the client doing all the listening. Cold reading can work under these circumstances, and indeed postal readings cannot work any other way. However, the cold reading process clearly works best if the client provides plenty of responses. For this reason, the psychic does whatever she can to make sure the reading becomes an interactive dialogue.

In this respect, some clients need less encouragement than others. Some confirmed believers are inclined to talk almost non-stop, thereby greatly facilitating the cold reading process. However, some clients are less generously forthcoming. They may be shy, wary, naturally reserved or sceptical. In these cases, the psychic has to work to overcome this reticence. There are many ways of doing this, some more subtle than others.

Prompts

A simple technique is for the psychic to provide plenty of feedback prompts, by which I mean conversational cues for the client to respond. We looked at a number of these in the section on 'Extracting information'. It also pays for the psychic to be a good listener who provides plenty of time for the client to talk openly, even if the client is not especially confident or articulate.

Open questions

Psychics also strive to make sure that they ask 'open' questions rather than 'closed' ones. This distinction will be familiar to anyone who knows about sales and inter-personal skills.

In case you have not met these terms before, closed questions are ones that can be answered 'yes/no' or 'agree/disagree'. They do not promote good interaction.

Open questions cannot be answered this way, and force the respondent to provide more detail. Open questions are much better for promoting and sustaining conversation. Here is a simple illustration of a closed question:

"Are you interested in music?"

The other person might simply say yes or no. There is no conversational flow, and it is then up to the first person to think of something else to say. Here is the open version:

"Tell me, what sort of music do you like?"

Now the other person has to think of more to say, and the conversation progresses beyond the rather banal level of 'yes/no' or 'agree/disagree'.

Eye contact

Psychics also promote responsiveness by making good use of direct eye contact. When you sustain direct eye contact with someone, you simultaneously (i) signal that you find them interesting, (ii) hold and guide their attention, and (iii) encourage them to pay attention to you. These three factors all encourage the other person to trust you and talk to you. Maintaining eye contact is not the same thing as staring, which has precisely the opposite effect.

Body language

I have already expressed my cautious stance towards the 'science' of body language. Nonetheless, if only for completeness, let me mention some body language factors that are theoretically relevant.

One is for the psychic to incline her head slightly left or right when listening to the client. According to body language theory, this signals a co-operative and consenting attitude, rather than one that is aggressive and confrontational. It therefore promotes the client's sense of security, and diminishes any confrontational aspect of the proceedings.

Venturing further into the realm of body language, the psychic may also take care to synchronise her own breathing pattern with that of the client. This is said to be a very subtle yet effective way to build a sense of rapport and mutual well-being.

Another is for the psychic to align her own posture with that of the client, so that they are not in what is called a 'crossing' or 'conflicting' position. In case the jargon is not clear enough, here is the theory. When you are talking to someone, imagine a line running across your body, connecting your shoulders. Imagine a similar line on the other person. The more parallel the lines, the more interested and sympathetic you seem to be to the other person. If the lines diverge or cross, this has the opposite effect.

I have tried the incline of the head and the posture alignment, and I can only report that they *seem* to work. Whether they *actually* work is for others to say.

So far, we have seen that the psychic can try numerous ways to encourage the client to provide feedback. The next question is, what types of feedback is she after?

Types of feedback

Clients can provide several different types of feedback. Obviously, the most direct kind is *verbal*. As well as listening to *what* the client says, the psychic also listens to:

— stress and emphasis

— tone and manner

Let us consider a simple response such as:

"I wouldn't say that was entirely true."

If you try saying this out loud, but emphasising a different word each time, you will see how this makes a difference to what the client means and what the psychic can therefore deduce.

I wouldn't say that was entirely true. (But others might, there are different viewpoints.)

I wouldn't say *that* was entirely true. (But other parts of what you've said seem accurate.)

I wouldn't say that was *entirely* true. (But you're more right than you are wrong.)

Even if the stress and emphasis is relatively even, the *manner* in which the client responds can reveal as much as the words themselves. Such factors as the client's phrasing, pace, tone of voice and confidence can all convey a great deal about what she is thinking and feeling.

A second important source of feedback is the client's *facial expression*. We all know from everyday life that this often provides many subtle clues to someone's thoughts. Similarly, subtle shakes and nods of the head can provide fairly clear signals to the attentive psychic.

A third source of feedback is provided by the client's *gestures and mannerisms,* such as scratching her ear or running her hand through her hair. Some cold reading sources set great store by this kind of feedback, and carefully list correlations between thought X and gesture Y. I consider this kind of 'analysis' to fall somewhere between idle fantasy and misleading exaggeration. Reliable evidence of such a close correlation is scarce. If a client scratches her nose, she may be signalling a lack of truthfulness but then again she may just have an itchy nose.

Clients generally remain blissfully unaware of the feedback they provide. In one demonstration I gave for BBC Television, the client maintained afterwards that she had tried hard not to give anything away. The video playback showed that she was nodding or shaking her head, giving me the plainest possible 'yes' or 'no' guidance, throughout the entire reading.

How psychics use feedback

Given that the psychic encourages feedback, and that it comes in several different forms, how does this assist the success of the psychic reading?

First of all, it helps the psychic to determine which of the Main Themes the client is most interested in. This strengthens the inexplicability of the process since it leaves the client wondering how the psychic knew that she was primarily concerned about her career or a relationship or money issues.

Secondly, it helps the psychic to gauge the extent to which the client agrees, or disagrees, with any statement she offers. The psychic capitalises on the strongest hits, and allows the misses to quietly fall by the wayside.

Perhaps most significantly, the different kinds of feedback help to reveal conflicts between what the client *says* and what she actually *feels.* This can be a very valuable aspect of cold reading. Clients often give responses that are less than honest, especially if something comes up that they consider embarrassing or sensitive. It can be very helpful for the psychic to perceive this.

Many clients leave a reading believing that they merely listened to a series of astonishing psychic revelations. They may never be aware that in fact they provided a glorious amount of information and feedback.

Sensory empathy

If there is one presentational technique that distinguishes the truly skilled cold reader from the rest, this is it. Sensory empathy is about the difference between merely *stating* something and actually *feeling* it — or at least pretending to do so.

When using this technique, the psychic acts if she can feel the same things the client feels. If she talks about the client being anxious, she acts as if she can 'feel' the same sort of anxiety. If she talks about the client's recent romantic happiness, she acts as if she 'feels' some of that same delight and happiness.

There are limits to how well this point can be conveyed in print, but let us look at an example. Consider a tarot reader who is offering a simple Greener Grass statement based on the choice between urban and rural life. It might sound like this:

> "In some ways the cards are telling a story of conflict and an inner restlessness. While you are quite well-adjusted to the hustle and bustle of city life, you have an affinity for the open air, the countryside and the chance to get away from it all.
>
> I sense you have given this some serious thought. You have often contemplated walking through leafy country lanes in the morning or enjoying the morning breeze coming in off the coast. I see times in the past when you have found yourself considering what your life might have been like outside the bright lights, the big city."

As a slice of typical psychic chatter, this is as good as it needs to be. The psychic can make it even more effective if she acts out a range of different *sensory impressions* matching what she says the client feels or has felt.

When the psychic mentions the client's 'inner restlessness', she can use her voice and facial expression to suggest she herself is *feeling* and *experiencing* what the client has felt and experienced.

When she says 'hustle and bustle', she could gesture as if clamping her hands flat over her ears to drown out the cacophony of sounds (street noises, traffic, sirens, phones ringing all day) that assault the client's hearing on a daily basis.

When she talks about 'the open air', she could perhaps close her eyes and breathe in deeply as if savouring the clean, invigorating air at the top of an Alpine peak.

When she refers to 'morning breeze coming in off the coast', she could look and sound as if she is inwardly transported to a bracing coastal region.

I am not suggesting the psychic throws herself around in a rather manic exhibition of erratic emotional display. This ruse can be subtle and still be highly effective. By seemingly experiencing the same sensations the client herself has experienced, the reading becomes much more captivating than it would be otherwise.

Cream principle

When you are adding cream to coffee, it is wise to start with just a little and then add more if you want. If you put too much in to begin with, you cannot get it out again. It is the same with cold reading statements. Psychics generally offer weak statements to begin with, rather than strong ones, because it is by far the safest strategy. For example, this is not good technique:

"You've had some major health problems with your back."

This is much better:

"I think you've had a little bit of back trouble now and again, haven't you?"

This element of caution gives the psychic two chances of being right. If the original, weak statement is correct, then it is a hit. On the other hand, if the client indicates that the original statement was not strong enough, the psychic makes the adjustment while sounding like she was correct all along:

"Well, that's putting it mildly. I've had several major back operations in my life."

"Yes, I could see it was a problem area. I didn't want to dwell on it too much, but nonetheless it's right isn't it?"

The psychic triumphs once again. Trying to turn a strong statement into a weak one sounds far less convincing. Unless it is done exceptionally well, it tends to sound false. Later in this book I quote one of my own early TV demonstrations in which I made this error. During the reading, I made initial statements that were far too bold and direct. In later readings I soon learned the benefit of using the Cream Principle.

Emphasising the conditional

Psychics place the emphasis on could / would / should statements that refer to possibilities, rather than facts. Why? Because then they *cannot* be wrong!

A moment's consideration should make this clear. If a client is told she is very creative, she may think this is true, or then again she may not. If she is told she *could* be very creative, or that she *should* be exploring her creative side more, there is no way for her to disagree. When you are merely being told what *could* be true, there is precious little scope for disagreement.

There are numerous constructions and expressions that turn an 'is' to a 'could be', and psychics use them all. For example, take this simple piece of Fine Flattery:

"You are very good with people, and know how to develop rapport."

This is a fairly safe piece of flattery, and few clients are going to offer any resistance to the idea. However, some unusually honest and self-critical clients might venture to disagree, and claim that they are terrible with people. In this situation, consider all these variants open to the psychic:

"You have the *potential* to be very good with people..."

"Aspects of your chart suggest you *might* well be good with people..."

"The impression I have is that you *ought to be* very good at handling people, given the right opportunity to develop this side of your character..."

"You *should* be very good with people. If you don't think you are, then something's blocking this potential within you..."

"You *could* be very good with people, but you have never really been given the chance to develop this side of your character."

These assertions can never be proved to be incorrect. Psychics know it is easy to take almost any piece of plain, factual observation and wrap it in the safety of a could / would / should statement.

Allowing for interpretation

In the course of a reading, the client often *hears* more detail than the psychic *provides*. Given rather bland statements that leave room for interpretation, the client will often supply extra details in her mind that render the statement more relevant to her own life. All the psychic has to remember to do is to allow for this phenomenon and not get in the way.

This is perhaps one of the strangest aspects of presentational technique. It means the psychic can enjoy credit for knowing something she doesn't actually know at all. Here is an example from one of my own readings:

> "And I think that two to three years ago there was at least one romantic line that became entangled."

At the time I offered this statement, I had no idea what relevance, if any, it would have for the client. Luckily for me, the client thought about it for a couple of seconds and then remembered an incident to which she felt this statement might apply. To this day, I have absolutely no idea what she was thinking about.

The client said I had described "exactly" what happened, adding that she preferred not to discuss it any further (the reading was being taped for television). In an apparently very gallant and sensitive manner, I agreed to say no more. In reality I hadn't a clue what was on her mind. As with all my TV demonstrations, the true extent of my psychic ability, by which I mean zero, was tactfully revealed to the client at a later stage in the show.

Clients provide this kind of supplementary detail both during the reading and after. Consider a simple Fuzzy Fact like this:

> "I see a process of transition that could be linked with the workplace."

This might later be remembered as follows:

> *"...she also told me I was going to be changing jobs soon, which is true because next month I'm taking over the new regional office."*

I have seen this happen on many occasions, with regard to my own readings and others. The psychic does not have to do anything to encourage this tendency. It happens quite naturally.

Forking

Forking means offering statements that can be developed in two different directions. If the client accepts the initial statement, then the psychic adds further embellishment. If the client rejects the initial statement, then the psychic drastically modifies it to make it more palatable. We looked at this technique briefly in connection with Barnum Statements. Here's an example:

> "You have a strong desire to be liked and admired, and seek credit for your achievements."

If the client agrees, the psychic develops this thread into something more substantial:

> "Sometimes this tendency to pursue approval may go a bit too far. If you're honest you know you sometimes come across as a little too keen for praise in the eyes of others. This is an area for growth and development. As you are learning, your own knowledge of your achievements matters more than what others say or think."

If the client disagrees, the psychic needs to reverse it to make it acceptable:

> "But you have learned to keep this tendency well hidden, so it's not something many would recognise in you. You often let the credit go elsewhere without making a fuss. You have learned not to get into acrimonious disputes about who deserves credit for what."

In this way, the psychic can always come out on top, no matter what sort of client she happens to be reading for at the time.

Forking and factual statements

It is easy to see that in terms of general character statements, forking is a very useful technique. It allows the psychic to always be right or mostly right. However, forking also allows the psychic to make direct factual assertions. Here is a trite example:

> "You used to own a dog."

If the client agrees, the psychic proceeds to say more about this delightful dog from days gone by. But what if the client rejects this statement? What if she never owned a dog? In this case, the psychic forks in the opposite direction: Here is one way she might do this:

> "Okay, I didn't mean you actually *owned* one as such. What I mean is that I sense you once *considered* owning a dog. It was on your mind, and you discussed it with someone."

This is the Interpretation revision that we saw in the section on 'The Win–Win Game'. Here is another option:

> "Well not a dog specifically. I didn't mean that. A dog was just the first thing that came to my mind. There was a domestic pet that meant a lot to you or your family, something you fussed over and liked."

The beautiful thing about forking is that it is entirely invisible. The client never knows what the psychic *would* have said if her own response had been different. This is what makes forking such a powerfully deceptive aspect of cold reading.

Psychics cannot use forking all the time with every element. It is far more effective if the psychic is content to let a few things go by as outright errors. For some reason, clients accept this as a by-product of the psychic process and tend to be very forgiving!

Keeping it clear

Like a good actor or presenter, the psychic tries to make sure that everything she says is clear and easily understood. This makes it easy to retain the client's concentration and attention, which in turn gives the psychic access to her responses. This is a simple aspect of presentation that applies as much to cold reading as it does to any other performing role.

Keeping it 'folksy'

Psychics know the value of keeping their readings informal in tone and easy to digest. We looked at this point earlier, in connection with the element I called 'Folk Wisdom'. This is obviously a matter of personal style, but in general psychics strive to keep their readings colourful, entertaining and easy to appreciate. They take care to express themselves using a vocabulary appropriate to the client, and to include figures of speech the client can relate to. This makes the experience easier to understand and encourages the client to join in.

Sustaining pace

Psychics know the value of sustaining a flowing, easy-going delivery. This allows the psychic to (a) get through plenty of different elements, waiting to see which ones are worth developing, and (b) smoothly get past misses and disagreements. It also means the client does not get too much time to analyse the reading's content.

Reprising with gold paint

This is another very important aspect of presentation, and one that has boosted the success of many psychic readings. It simply involves the psychic reviewing and revising each section of the reading in a manner that is heavily biased in her own favour. This affects what the client remembers of the reading. Take this example:

"I sense that when you were quite young you had quite a serious accident, possibly involving water. Can you make some sense of this for me?"

"Not really. There was something along those lines, but I wasn't really very young at the time."

In essence, the client has rejected the statement. However, she has hinted that a past event could provide at least a partial match. The psychic now uses a standard manoeuvre to get around this miss, such as the Focus revision (see the earlier section on 'The Win–Win Game'). At the same time, she forks away from her initial statement with a little light humour:

"Well, something that happened when you were younger than you are now, we can agree on that!"

"Yes, of course..."

"And what I'm getting is an accident, an illness, something that laid you low for a while or had those around you worried. It's a very strong impression indeed."

"Yes, well if it's what I think it is, it was a car accident. But I was the cause, not the victim. I was about 19 and I hadn't been driving long."

Now the psychic is more or less home and dry. The client has provided details about an event that bears very little relation to the psychic's original offering. The psychic builds on this information, and at the same time starts introducing the Reprise:

"So, this car accident that I saw in your youth — I get the sense that you learned some lessons that are still with you today. Lessons about responsibility, and the need to mix caution with confidence. I feel this has been an important area of growth for you, which could be why I got such a strong impression along these lines..."

In this reprise, the psychic has managed to make two references to having accurately picked up on this car accident from years ago. In fact, she never mentioned a car and clearly was not referring to the client's late teenage years. When the client thinks back over the reading, and when she tells others about it, she may well retain the impression that the psychic knew all about this particular incident and mentioned many specific details.

Rapid reprise

Reprising with Gold Paint can be used in many psychic readings, and does not have to take a long time. It can be accomplished in the blink of an eye. To see what I mean, imagine a psychic is giving a spiritualist reading. Furthermore, suppose she has guessed, incorrectly, that the person 'in spirit' is *not* a relative of the client, but a close personal friend instead. The psychic might say something like:

> "And this person who's coming through, this is someone who you were very close to for many years, and you had a lot of good times together, isn't that right?"
>
> *"Well, if it's the person I'm thinking of, it's my father."*
>
> "Oh well in that case you certainly were very close weren't you? So this is making sense to you isn't it?"
>
> *"Yes it is."*
>
> "I thought so, and what your father is telling me is that he remembers playing with you on a holiday you had that was near the beach..."

The psychic has quietly shifted from 'someone you were very close to' to 'your father', but only *after* the client provided this identification. The psychic's original vagueness (or error, depending how you look at it) is quietly left to wilt on the vine of forgetfulness. The client takes away the impression that the psychic had identified her father before she said a word. This is not what happened, but it is how it will be remembered.

Summarising the reading

At the end of the reading, if circumstances permit, experienced psychics try to conclude with a brief summary of the territory covered. This is another chance to include some of the biased revision mentioned earlier, under 'Reprise with Gold Paint'. It allows the psychic to emphasise the parts that went well, and to gloss over those that were less successful. This affects how the client remembers the reading, which in turn affects how she describes it to others. This is all part of building a successful reputation.

It is widely acknowledged by people who have looked into this area that clients generally remember their readings inaccurately. I myself have seen clients refer enthusiastically to details in my own readings that were never actually there.

Looking good for the crowd

So far, this section has focused on presentational techniques that enhance the reading in the eyes of the client. There is one more presentational technique that is aimed at *onlookers*, rather than the client herself.

Psychics often give readings in circumstances where other people can *see* what is going on although they cannot hear what is being said. For example at corporate parties or fairgrounds, people can sometimes see the psychic and her current client facing one another without being able to hear the confidential brilliance being shared. In these circumstances, it looks very impressive if people see that the client is nodding and agreeing a great deal. It creates the impression that the psychic is dispensing many pearls of wisdom.

However, the client's conspicuous nodding and signs of agreement may have nothing to do with the content of the reading. The psychic may simply be peppering her reading with *nodding prompts*. These include phrases such as, "Can you hear what I'm saying?" / "Can you hear me all right?" / "Can you understand me?"

We have already seen how important it is for the psychic to keep her reading clear and audible. However, the psychic can do this and at the same time employ a *relatively* soft tone of voice, supposedly in the spirit of confidentiality. If she does this, and sprinkles her reading with nodding prompts, the client can be made to nod her head as if she were avidly watching an international yo-yo competition.

From a little distance away, this creates the perfect illusion of the client firmly endorsing every shimmering utterance that falls from the psychic's lips. This is very good for trade.

Progress Review

Section Two is sub-divided into seven sections, and so far we have covered five of them. First, we looked at The Set Up, or how the psychic tries to get the conditions right for a successful reading. Next, we looked at the actual content of the reading itself: the Main Themes and Main Elements. Each element provides a different way of saying something that sounds suitably psychic in nature, without any need for real psychic faculties.

We have also looked at the Win–Win Game, or how psychics cover up mistakes during the reading. In the most recent section, we considered the different aspects of Presentation that are also part and parcel of the cold reading process.

The next area to consider is how all these methods and techniques are stitched together into a psychic reading.

How CR Works 6/7: Putting It All Together

The psychic toolbox

An experienced builder has a good set of tools that enable him to cope with most situations. The more different tools he has, the greater the range of jobs he can handle. There may be some tools that he trusts and relies on more than others, and his preferences will reflect his own individual style of working.

Likewise with the psychic. The techniques and elements we have looked at so far are a sort of 'psychic toolbox' that can be used to construct readings. It makes no sense to use *every* tool for *every* reading. All the psychic has to do is use the right tools at the right time to deliver a successful reading for each client. The more tools the psychic has at her disposal, the more versatile she is and the more clients she can impress and satisfy.

So the first point to emphasise is that 'putting it all together' is very much a case of personal style and can vary tremendously from one psychic to the next.

Almost improvising

Putting it all together is also largely a matter of *improvisation*. Before the psychic begins the reading, she may have only the vaguest idea of what she is going to say. This is not a problem. Provided she has a good repertoire of techniques and elements at her disposal, she should be able to cope with just about any client she meets.

Nonetheless, very few readings are *totally* improvised. Every cold reader has a few elements, or a few statements, that have become favourites over time and that she tends to use more than others. Of course, this will not be obvious to any individual client. It would only become clear if one were able to study many readings given by the same psychic over a period of time.

Principal phases

Given that readings vary according to personal style, and are generally improvised rather than scripted, there is no one way to 'put it all together' and fashion a psychic reading. However, the majority of normal one-on-one readings can be said to proceed through the same five main phases:

- Set Up & Disarm
- Launch
- Bridge
- Expand
- Tidy Conclusion

I will describe each one, and add some notes from my own experience of giving readings.

Set Up and Disarm

To begin with, the psychic employs whichever 'Set Up' techniques are appropriate to the psychic's style, the client, and the context of the reading. It is obviously up to the psychic to choose the techniques she feels will be most effective, based on her own experience. She must also be on the alert for any potential problems, such as a very hostile or sceptical client, and defuse them.

In my own readings, I generally tend to focus on just two 'Set Up' techniques: encouraging co-operative interpretation, which I regard as more or less essential, and establishing the belief system. In addition, I always watch for signs of either nervousness or a sceptical attitude.

If the client seems nervous, it is clearly important to set her at ease. I try to ascertain why she is nervous, simply by asking about this in a sympathetic way. Not only is this conducive to a successful reading, it can also yield good clues as to the direction the reading should take.

Whatever the client says, I take care to provide the reassurances she requires. If she's worried about me seeing 'bad things', as many are, I mention that all my readings are about good news and positive trends in life.

If the client is suspicious or sceptical, I tend to play down the belief system (since this can only invite confrontation) and talk about the reading in more rational terms. For example, I might suggest that readings are akin to the exploration of psychological trends and archetypes, or that they constitute a form of intuitive counselling and advice in which the props (tarot cards, astrological data etc.) are just a means to an end. It is really just a case of saying whatever I feel might disarm, or diminish, the client's sceptical stance.

Launch

Next, the psychic has to actually start the reading. It is important for the reading to get off to a good start, and for this reason few psychics rely *purely* on improvised cold reading at this early stage. Most have a few phrases they have learned to trust or an introductory framework they have polished over time. These tried-and-tested opening lines help the psychic to sound proficient, experienced and, most importantly of all, supremely confident.

Confidence is contagious. This important point doesn't just apply to psychic readings. It applies to any kind of live performance. When a performer takes to the stage looking and sounding confident, the audience can sense it. They soon relax, because they feel that the performer knows what he or she is doing. Because they relax, they respond more easily and enthusiastically. They applaud more at the end of each song or laugh more at each joke. The performer can sense the supportive atmosphere and gets the feeling that things are going well. This, in turn, helps him or her to relax and give a great performance. Because the performance is so good, the audience are even more appreciative... and so the virtuous circle goes round.

Lack of confidence is also contagious, and has precisely the opposite effect. The performer takes to the stage and looks nervous and ill-prepared. The audience quickly become tense (or bored). They think, "This doesn't look like it's going to be any good." Because they are tense, they don't respond much. The performer senses this lack of warmth and response and becomes more nervous. This tends to make the performance even worse, so the audience enjoy it even less... and the vicious circle is complete.

This is why confidence is vitally important to any kind of performance, including cold reading. Unfortunately, confidence is not to be had just for the wanting. It only comes with experience.

In terms of starting a reading, my own preference is to find some pretext for going back in time and starting with the client's younger days. More or less any pretext will do, so long as it is vaguely appropriate to the context of the reading. Having started in this way, I then rely chiefly on a partially pre-set spiel that includes Fuzzy Facts and Childhood Memories. This provide my first few minutes of material. If it is difficult or inappropriate to go back in time, I tend to rely on a very safe yet potent cocktail of Jacques and Fine Flattery statements to get things under way.

Bridge

Next, the psychic has to find a way to bridge from the start of the reading (only partially improvised) to the main body of the reading (almost entirely improvised). In this respect, she has two main goals. The first is to touch on each of the Principal Themes to see which ones appear most important to the client. The second is to include two or three elements aimed at extracting information if she has not already done so.

Establishing which main theme to pursue is obviously important. Many clients come to a reading seeking help or advice about one specific matter. If the psychic manages to focus on the right area, this makes a good impression. On the other hand, if she talks at length about matters of little interest to the client, then the client will naturally be dissatisfied.

When it comes to extracting information, my two favourite elements tend to be the Veiled Question and the Jargon Blitz.

Expand

The psychic is now in a good position to improvise the main body of the reading, using whichever elements she prefers. She knows which theme(s) to emphasise, and she has extracted at least one or two crumbs of information that she can put to good use. With any luck, she has already successfully conditioned the client to co-operate with the process and to accept unquestioningly the strange rules by which the game is played.

In my own readings, I tend to rely chiefly on Rainbow Ruse and Greener Grass statements. I also try to hit specific names, numbers and other details likely to impress the client, using Fuzzy Facts and the Good Chance Guess. In almost every reading I chance my arm with at least one Lucky Guess and at least one Push Statement.

As the reading unfolds, the psychic gains feedback from the client all the time. This of course greatly influences the direction the reading takes. At any time, the psychic can try to extract more feedback from the client to gain more clues as to the best direction to go in. In this regard, I tend to rely on the Russian Doll and the Jargon Blitz.

This process of ongoing improvisation may sound rather risky and insecure. It is as well to bear in mind that psychics give readings all the time, whereas clients only have readings once in a while. Hence in any given reading, all the experience and readiness is on the side of the psychic. It is her game, and it is played by her rules. If a particular part of the reading is not going well, the psychic knows she can always cut that part short and start talking about something else. If the client becomes difficult or awkward, the psychic can spot this at once and deal with it effectively.

Tidy Conclusion

As you would expect, predictions about the future tend to come towards to end of the reading. In this regard, I usually play quite safe and use Pollyanna Pearls. The final phase of the reading consists of summarising all that has been said, in the rather biased manner described earlier, and bidding the client farewell with every good wish for the future.

That is more or less all there is to it! Another reading over, another satisfied client.

Progress Review

We have now covered six of Section Two's seven sub-sections. We have seen in some detail how cold reading works, from start to finish.

There are really only two ways in which the cold reading process can fail. One is if the client is well-versed in cold reading and knows how to block it. This is the subject of Section Four. The other is if the client is thoroughly sceptical. However, there are ways of handling this, as we will see in the next section.

How CR Works 7/7: Handling Sceptics

It is rare for a psychic to meet a client who is both sceptical and well-informed. Most clients are either believers or non-committal. Even the few that may come along with a sceptical attitude tend to know nothing about cold reading and can therefore be taken in by the process just like anyone else.

However, even if someone sceptical and well-informed *does* turn up, this is not a problem for any psychic with a little bit of experience. She can cope quite easily. Here are some of the best lines of defence when sceptics appear.

Making no claim

One of the first things the psychic can do is try to disarm the sceptic. A good way to do this is to say that she makes no claims, and asks the client to believe in nothing. The guiding principle here is that a claim that is not made is a claim that cannot be disproved. A typical riff on these lines might go like this:

> "Let me say right at the start that I myself make no claims on behalf of the tarot (or astrology, etc.). All I can tell you is that many people find it a useful way of enhancing their perspective on life, and perhaps opening a window to a broader appreciation of the cycles and themes in life that affect us all one way or another. That's really all there is to it, and all I ask of you is that you keep an open mind, enjoy the reading and see how it can be of benefit to you."

A neat little opening speech along these lines is a very cute way to defuse all possible sceptical challenges. The psychic cannot fail to deliver on her promises because she has been careful not to make any. Nor has she made any promises on behalf of her particular discipline. She has not said it will reveal truths, solve problems or prove anything at all. Given that nothing has been defined as a successful outcome, nothing can constitute an unsuccessful one either.

The psychic industry has the best client contracts of all time: 'You pay me, and I promise nothing in return'. I suggest this should be regarded as a consumer rights issue, in which case the appropriate response is:

> *"If you're not promising anything, then what am I paying for?"*

Praising the caution

Another good disarming move is to *praise* the client's caution, and to *express* *approval* for her reluctance to embrace the psychic system on offer. Many psychics like to recycle neat little anecdotes about how they too are of a very sceptical cast of mind, and only accepted astrology (tarot / palmistry / reading entrails) because they discovered that it really does work. Here is how an astrologer might go about doing this:

"I can sense a degree of very healthy scepticism in you, and let me say I absolutely applaud it. Believe me, no-one's more sceptical than I am! After all, there's a lot to be sceptical about these days, isn't there?

Let me just say one thing. The only reason I became an astrologer was because I discovered for myself that it does work and it really is useful. That's what my clients tell me as well. It's the oldest science we have, and in some ways a very rational person like yourself stands to gain more from it than anyone else. So, let's get started shall we..."

And so the reading can begin. This preliminary spiel might not have any effect, but it will certainly not do any harm. At the very least, it stands a chance of building a degree of rapport.

Offering sugar lumps

Earlier in this book, in the section labelled 'Elements about character', we looked at Sugar Lump statements. These statements offer the client a pleasant emotional reward in return for believing in whatever psychic nonsense is on offer. These kinds of statements are also used to try and soften sceptical attitudes.

I first learned about Sugar Lump statements by being on the receiving end of one. I once attended a psychic fair (or 'fayre') and paid for a tarot reading out of idle curiosity. I was implored to 'open my heart as well as my mind' to the 'warmth, love and guidance' that the psychic community can offer. I was also urged to avail myself of the 'very real contribution' that psychic insights can make towards achieving my goals in life.

I had my doubts at the time, and I still have them today. I am lucky enough to have plenty of warmth and love in my life, and I do not get it from highly irrational women wearing tacky pendants and too much make-up. As for my goals in life, I felt relatively safe ignoring long-term career advice from someone whose professional skill base consisted of serving up superstitious drivel while peering at some cards based on medieval artwork.

Giving up

Simply giving up may sound like a rather desperate and pathetic tactic, but in the psychic industry it's a perfectly legitimate move. What's more, it can be achieved without any loss of face whatsoever.

If all else fails, and the psychic feels she is having a hard time, her simplest option is to stop the reading, refund the money and move on to the next client who has 'gullible, vulnerable and highly co-operative' stamped on her forehead. It might sound something like this:

> "I can only report what I feel, and in truth I don't feel that you are sufficiently receptive to what the tarot has to offer for the reading to be a good use of either your time or mine. I am sorry about this, but I don't feel I'm the right reader for you, and this being the case I feel the time has come to say the reading is over."

Another variation is to blame lack of rapport:

> "I want to be honest with you, and say that the success of any reading has a lot to do with the rapport between myself and whoever I'm reading for. I haven't felt able to develop the right kind of rapport with you that is so important for a successful and productive reading. This isn't a criticism of you personally, but I don't feel I'm able to provide the sort of reading I'd feel was worth the time, and intuitive effort, that is involved."

The more confrontational approach is to suggest that sceptical attitudes themselves are somehow responsible for inhibiting or blocking psychic gifts:

> "At this point I would like to end the sitting. You have made it clear that you are highly sceptical, and although that's your right, I honestly feel that your scepticism is preventing the consultation from being effective. My kind of psychic sensitivity takes years to develop. If you are unsympathetic to this sensitivity, as I feel you are, this blocks the channels that are vital to my work and through which I was trying to help you. So if you'll excuse me, the reading is over."

Whichever approach the psychic uses, she is able to end the reading, cut her losses and move on. She can blame the failure on the client's attitude, bad vibrations, blocked channels, the configuration of the stars or anything else that comes to mind.

The other faintly possible explanation, that the whole thing could be a heap of superstitious claptrap, is generally not mentioned.

Progress Review

In Section Two, the lengthiest in the book, we have seen how cold reading works, and shown how adaptable it can be. Having dealt with the theory, it is time to see some cold reading in action, which is the subject of Section Three. But first, a brief Interlude.

Interlude: On Explaining Miracles

I with was some friends the other day when one of them mentioned a psychic reading he once had. This happens to me quite often. I usually want to talk about the important things in life such as Jacqueline Bisset, great guitar music or the frustrating search for excellent fajitas in London. My friends, being sadly less interested in such matters but aware of my interests, often prefer to discuss tales of psychic miracles.

As occupational hazards go, it is not the worst I can think of. Besides, I am the first to admit that tales of psychic powers can be fun and intriguing. Nonetheless, I still wince inwardly whenever this happens. There are two reasons.

The first is that every such tale tends to be markedly similar to the last one I heard, and the one before that, and the two before that, and the ten before that... and so on. The second reason is that one particular phrase *always* crops up at the end of these stories. Let me share it with you.

My friend's story was about a psychic he saw early one year, before he had planned his holidays. During the reading, the psychic said my friend would go on holiday in October. Sure enough, October came round and he went on holiday. As far as my friend was concerned, this was evidence of uncanny psychic ability. Having finished his story, my friend sipped his drink and then said, "So how do you explain that?"

That's the phrase. I can see it coming from miles away, and I groan to myself whenever it looms on the horizon. May I take this opportunity to explain why.

Explaining things away

In the first place, I am not remotely interested in trying to 'explain things away', and nor is any other sceptic I have ever met. For me, being sceptical boils down to one thing: I like to believe in things that are true, and to avoid believing in things that turn out to be nonsense. As human beings, we are all prone to believing in rubbish, and life is not short of temptations and opportunities to do so. Fortunately, there are some good ways of reducing the likelihood of this happening. Asking good questions is one. Getting well-informed about things is another. Trying to learn about good and bad reasoning is yet another.

I have tried to learn a few of these methods, and to apply them in everyday life. This does not make life boring, or soul-less, or devoid of joy, excitement, warmth and fun (if anything, quite the reverse). It just means I do not make quite as many dumb mistakes as I probably would otherwise. This is what I think it means to be 'sceptical'.

A question of recall

In the second place, it is worth looking at this whole business of being asked to 'explain' things. Like anyone else, I can only explain something if I can get at the facts, and a story told over a drink or two at the bar is not a set of facts. It is a recollection. A view. An impression of what someone *thinks* happened. Of course, my friend felt sure he knew *exactly* what happened during the reading, and *exactly* what was said. Alas, his confidence was probably misplaced.

Accurate recall is prone to at least four kinds of contamination. Generally speaking:

- people are not very good at *observing* things very accurately
- what little they observe well, they are not very good at *remembering* very accurately
- what little they remember well, they are not very good at *describing* very accurately to others
- and what little they describe well, they tend to *simplify*

If you doubt the above is true, have a look at the formal academic research that has been done in this area. There is a lot of it, and it all points the same way: the human mind is wonderful in countless ways, but next to hopeless at accurately describing past experience.

If you do not care to check out the research, and I do not blame you, just try out your friends and family. Ask them to recall the opening words of the TV sitcom they have just watched. They probably won't have the faintest idea. If you have been talking to a friend for ten minutes face-to-face, ask them to close their eyes and describe what you are wearing. Very few will be able to remember the details (although women will do better than men).

Many people cannot even say with certainty whether the numerals on their own watch are regular 'Arabic' style (1, 2, 3) or Roman (I, II, III). Or which way the head faces on their country's coins and stamps. Try asking people to describe basic details of pictures that hang on their own walls and that they see every day. Most people cannot even recall the opening words of this paragraph (no cheating!).

This is no great disgrace. Most of us have never developed great powers of accurate recall because we do not need to. Life is complicated enough, and we take in just enough details to get by. I do it myself, and you probably do too.

The fallibility of human recall is not the problem. The problem is the lack of *awareness* of this fallibility. When people adamantly insist that they can remember something very well, they are usually wrong. This gives rise to difficulties. In relationships, it gives rise to rows about past conversations (the 'That's *not* what I said!' syndrome). In law, it gives rise to flawed eyewitness testimony. In many other fields it causes all sorts of strife, conflicts, confusions and difficulties. All these problems would vanish if people could just acknowledge that what they *think* happened may not be what actually *did* happen. This applies to sceptics just as much as to anyone else. It's just that sceptics are probably more aware of the fact than most.

Trained observers?

In some instances, defenders of psychic phenomena contend that a particular witness is more credible than average, since he or she is professionally trained to be a good observer. This may be true, but only up to a point.

Someone may have very good observational skills *in their own field of expertise*, but these skills do not necessarily translate to situations outside their professional domain. Doctors are trained to make good observations of patients and their symptoms. Police officers are trained to observe crime scenes accurately. However, in other contexts these people may be no more accurate than average, which is to say not very accurate at all.

Taped readings?

In the case of psychic readings, many clients these days come away with a recording of what took place. (Quite a few psychics offer to record readings for a small extra fee.) This merely relocates the problem, rather than eliminating it. A client may possess a recording of the reading, but how accurately does she recall and describe its contents when talking to her friends? There is no way of knowing.

Nor can a recording tell us about many factors that *may* have been involved in the reading such as prior information, visual clues and non-verbal client feedback.

Summary

To recap, when we hear someone describing what happened to them, we are usually getting a *simplified* account, not very well *described*, of something not very well *remembered*, of something not very well *observed* in the first place.

So how did the psychic predict my friend's October holiday? The answer is that I do not know if she did, and if she did I have no idea how. Perhaps it was an astonishing demonstration of authentic psychic precognition. Then again, maybe the psychic was as genuine as a 7 dollar bill and my friend was suckered by a piece of stylish cold reading. I was not there, and I have no way of finding out the facts that would inform my judgement either way. More to the point, I cannot get at the facts by listening to my friend's *recollection* of what took place.

It is impossible to 'explain' an anecdote. Even if it were possible, it is not what scepticism is all about.

Time, I feel, to get down off my soapbox and back to the subject of cold reading.

Section 3: Demonstrations

"For the great majority of mankind are satisfied with appearance, as though they were realities, and are often more influenced by the things that seem than those that are."

- Niccolo Machievelli, 'Discourses'

From tarot to astrology

This section features two examples from my televised demonstrations of cold reading. In the first, I was asked to pose as a tarot reader, and in the second as an astrologer. Both of these demonstrations were given for British TV. I will also refer to a third demonstration, for American TV, in which I posed as a clairvoyant.

Two points about me

My involvement with cold reading sometimes gives rise to two unhelpful misunderstandings. This seems like a good opportunity to clear them up.

The first misunderstanding is that I am psychic. This means I often get letters from people who mistakenly think I can help them run their lives. I have been asked about romantic partners, exam questions and missing pets. I cannot help with any of these things because I am as psychic as a teapot. Maybe less.

The second misunderstanding is that I am some sort of con-artist. This means I get delightful letters from that very special community of people whose hobby is being angry about things they know nothing about. These pious, lovely people traduce me for my callous practices and vent their outrage at my wicked ways. It's a great way to start Monday mornings.

I am not a con-artist. Among other things, I am a lecturer and entertainer with an interest in what *real* mind power is all about. For various reasons, including a well-spent youth, I happen to know about deception and how to fake psychic phenomena. In my shows, I often demonstrate a wide range of seemingly psychic phenomena, from spoon-bending to ESP. However, I always stress that I am an entertainer, not a psychic.

Sometimes, media people ask me to demonstrate that cold reading really works. They find someone willing to have a reading, and I strut my stuff. Afterwards, the person to whom I have given the reading is told the truth as tactfully and sensitively as possible. I also make it clear to the client that having being taken in by cold reading does not mean she is gullible or lacking in intelligence.

Test conditions

The purpose of these demonstrations was to see if I could convince a complete stranger that I was genuinely psychic, purely by using cold reading. The majority of my TV demonstrations have been conducted under what I refer to as 'test conditions'. Let me explain what this actually means.

1. The TV people select the clients for the readings, and I have no say in their choice. All I usually ask is that the clients should be female, in the age range 21-55, since in real life most clients fall into this category.

2. I do not know the identity of the clients until the moment the readings begin, and I have no prior information about them. Even when I am eventually introduced to them, all I am told is their first name.

3. Care is taken to choose clients who have no *strong* opinions about psychic ability either way (some have turned out to be mild believers, others mildly sceptical).

4. The clients are not told anything favourable about my abilities or otherwise conditioned to believe in me. All they are told is that I am going to give them a reading, and that they will be asked for their honest comments afterwards.

5. The reading has to last at least 20 minutes. It has to be reasonably detailed, and more than just a string of bland Barnum Statements.

6. Once the reading is over the client is to be interviewed separately, with no further involvement on my part. The client is to be asked for her honest opinion, without being prompted to say anything favourable. In the course of the interview, the client will be asked specifically to consider if I might have been some sort of fake.

7. I only have one chance to give each reading, without rehearsal, re-takes or breaks. I agree to the results being broadcast whatever the outcome.

8. I insist that after the reading and the interview, the truth is explained to the client as sensitively and inoffensively as possible without making her feel gullible or foolish. She is to be told I am a fake (if she has not already come to this conclusion) and to have the purpose of the experiment explained to her in full.

Transcripts

At the beginning of Section Two, I emphasised that the examples in that section were purely hypothetical. In contrast, the examples in this section are genuine transcripts of actual readings I have given for television, and of the client's subsequent reactions.

Real conversational speech is neither as simple nor as tidy as fictional dialogue. In real life, people leave their thoughts incomplete, repeat themselves, mumble, mutter and offer disjointed phrases. For all these reasons, a literal transcript can be difficult to read. Please bear this in mind.

I have made the transcripts as accurate and complete as I can. I have made very minor edits only where the original words, or fragments of words, would be impenetrably confusing. However, I have not cheated or made any misleading edits. I have neither omitted the 'misses', nor made the 'hits' look better than they really were.

Example 1: Improvised tarot reading

Introduction

This first example is taken from a TV series called 'The Talking Show', made by Open Media Productions for Channel 4 Television, a national terrestrial TV channel in the UK. The Open Media team were a pleasure to work with from start to finish, and I would like to pay tribute to all their hard work and professionalism in making this interesting experiment possible.

For this demonstration, the producers asked me to pose as a tarot reader, and to improvise the reading in a television studio. There was no studio audience present at the time. They were shown edited tapes of the readings later as part of the actual show.

The client

The client for this first example turned out to be a young woman called Susie, in her late twenties or early thirties. She was tall, slim, well-dressed and very well-spoken. She came across as being well-educated, pleasant, and quite interested in the reading although not particularly co-operative. At first meeting she appeared rather solemn, but in the early stages of the reading it became clear she had a very likeable sense of humour. Although she was responsive, she was not very talkative. She generally offered only very brief, monosyllabic responses.

The reading

Here is a complete transcript of the reading I gave to Susie.

- - -

Me: "Your name is?"

Susie: "Susie."

"Is that short for...?"

"Susan."

"...Susan or Susannah?"

"Susan."

"Okay. Let's talk about what we're going to do today. The first thing is I'd like to know if you've had a reading done before."

"Never."

"Never? Is this because you don't believe or you..."

"Er, I suppose there's never been one [a tarot reader] around when I've thought about it! Er, I don't believe or not believe."

"Okay, that's what we call an open mind."

"An open mind, yeah."

"Well, what I'd like you to do... not that you're here to do things for me, I'm going to try and do my best for you..."

"Okay."

"...what I'd like you to do is to forget about all these people [the TV crew] who are watching us and listening. We won't go into anything that's too private. We won't go into any bad news or anything like that. The first thing I'd like to do, is just explain that the cards will be your cards."

"Right."

"What they mean will probably mean more to you than to me."

"Yep."

"But I will do what I can for you."

"Uh-huh." [understanding and agreeing]

"The first thing I'd like you to do is just hold the cards for a while, while you think about the things that are uppermost in your mind and in your heart and in your life at the moment.

You can take your time to do this. Again, it's part of relaxing and not worrying about all these people around us. And then, if you would just put the cards down and then cut a pile off."

"What, so we've got two piles?"

"That's right, yes. Just put the cards down... and cut them for me."

" [Performing the procedure] Like that?"

"Okay, that's fine. [I laid out three banks of six cards each, for past present and future respectively. Initially only the first set were face up.] And we'll take some of the cards here for the past, and then we'll do some in the middle which we'll turn over in a second, and then we'll have a look at Susie's future. I need one more, could you just cut again? That's fine. I'll just move these [the superfluous cards] out of the way.

Okay. So what we're going to try and do is first of all find a little bit about where you've been, so to speak, in the past and we could be looking back quite a way away. I'm quite happy with some of the cards that I see. There's no need to agree or disagree with anything."

"Uh-huh." [agreement and understanding]

"Obviously it's going to be more out of focus for me than it is for you..."

"Sure."

"... and some of the time, if we want to go into a particular theme, it wouldn't hurt for you to tell me if there's something that connects here.

Okay, the nice thing is we're getting The Magician and the King of Wands and the Nine of Wands [showing Susie some of the cards] and things like that, which are very much to do with someone who is driven by her own volition, not pushed around by other people.

Somebody who works hard for the things she gets in life. Somebody who plans ahead, who works things out, and who isn't just somebody who's pushed around or at the beck and call of other people. And I think that if you're honest, and if someone were to put this to you, that through your life you can say that you've encountered an awful lot of objections, and barriers, and people saying no, and problems, but you can overcome them."

"Uh, yeah."

"It's not that I think you fit some awful stereotype of being bossy and pushy, because I really don't think that's you, [light-hearted tone] although I'm sure we could probably round up two or three people who think you are!"

[laughter, nodding and agreement] "Yes, maybe some [would] agree with that!"

"But actually if were looking at the inner you, I don't think that is you. But you are somebody who has worked hard for the things that you have got. You're not somebody where things just fall into your lap."

[laughter and emphasis that this is certainly not the case] "No!"

"That's quite a ridiculous idea for you isn't it? We all know people who are like that, they're born with a silver spoon and everything just goes right for them. But I think you're more the sort of person who has... you've met the objections, and you've met the barriers and the blocks and the negatives, but you overcome."

"Right."

"The other thing... we're going to touch on quite a few different aspects of your life..."

"Yeah."

"... I think that there's a sign here that says that when you were quite young, and you may have go back quite some time, I'm picking up an impression from some of the cards I get, I could be wrong, but I think there was an accident when you were quite young. Your family and your parents and... do you have brothers and sisters...?"

"One of each."

"...one of each, I thought so, and they will have talked about this, and it happened when you were quite young. There was an accident, it was something there are no visible scars today but you took quite a knock at the time. Does this make sense for you?"

"Yes. I wouldn't quite call it an accident, but yes, when I was quite young."

"A mishap."

"A mishap, yes."

"Were you more... is it true to say... I'm getting the impression that your family, particularly your parents, were more concerned than they had need to be at the time because in the end it didn't turn out to be as serious as they thought."

"Yeah, possibly."

"Okay, so that's that. The nice thing about that is that some of the things we see here [the cards representing the past] I will also pick up impressions of here in the present."

"Okay."

"But that [the accident/mishap] is firmly behind you. It's definitely over your shoulder, so it's not one of these things that's a lingering influence."

"Yep."

"Let's come forward a little bit in time. There are some nice cards. We've got the Ace of Cups, we've got the Two of Cups. Cups are to do with possessions and Cups are to do with things that you own. There is, if I may say so, and I'm aware there are people watching this, there is a materialist side to you. If you're being honest..."

[laughs a little] "Yep."

"... but I don't think you would say it's the most governing influence in you."

"No."

"And I guess we all know some people, they're admirable because they're not materialist at all and they seem quite happy and content in a dustbin. To be honest you're not like that."

"No."

"I think that earlier on in life, there's... [hesitating] you see, when we have some of these symbols here there's a contrast... there is a creative talent here."

"Yes."

"That's part of here [the past] and of here [the present]. I don't like to start making guesses 'cos it looks phoney..."

"Sure."

"...but let me tell you the impression I get."

"Okay."

"The impression I get is that when you were very young people knew you had quite a striking talent or ambition in one... I don't think, although you have an aesthetic sense and an artistic sense, I don't think it's in that area. I think it could be more to do with very much the subject that our friends here [the TV producers] are concerned with, communication and words. But we'll come on to that in a second."

"Yeah." [understanding the process]

"Now I think this is a talent that you had the scope to develop. And I don't think this is something that's just been left in the past, but we'll

---

140

come on to that later. But I think at the moment it would be true to say you haven't had the opportunity to develop this talent in the way that perhaps some people, your parents or friends or teachers thought you would at the time.

It's the sort of thing where people said 'Oh that's going to take Susie a long way, that's going to be...' but in fact that didn't happen. And at the moment it's not something that you're capitalising on. Does this make sense to you?"

"Yes."

"Okay. That's fine. I want to move on and sort of wind the clock forward a little bit and perhaps talk about teenage years and early relationships and this sort of thing. It's very difficult, but I like to try and do it because if it works it's fun for me and it's fun for you."

"Okay, yeah."

It's difficult to get impressions of letters, but I think that if you look back, there's nothing sort of flirtatious about this, you had a few relationships in your teenage years...!" [light-hearted tone, suggesting significant numbers]

"Yes." [laughter]

"You know, it wasn't just sort of one off..."

"Right." [laughter]

"I think you can remember somebody er, [hesitation] I'm getting the sound of an 'M' or an 'N', it could be a 'Nick' or a 'Mick', one of those diminutives, meant something to you."

[Puzzled, little response]

"Will you think about that if it doesn't actually make sense for you right now?"

"Okay."

"This was somebody that you knew perhaps in connection with your education. It could be within the school area, a boyfriend, or somebody that you were close to, a good friend. It need not have been someone you were going out with. I get the impression that we're talking about that sort of sound, 'Nick' or 'Mick' or that could have just been a diminutive that they used. Can you find somebody like that?"

"Not really, no..."

"That's not a problem..."

"I've got a brother called Michael but that's about as far..."

"...uh-huh? But were you quite close?"

"Reasonably."

"Reasonably close, more so... I mean, we all know families where sadly there's not really a lot of communication. It could be that's what I'm getting."

"Mmm." [agreement]

"I'll be honest with you, and be honest enough to admit it, I didn't think it was a family connection because I tend to work away from that, tend to look outwards..."

"Somewhere else, right..."

"...but just trying to pick up on what I'm getting and what's making sense to you, would it be fair to say that at the time I was trying to look at, which was..."

"Teenage years." [agreeing and following the reprise]

"...the teenage years, that relationship you had with your brother — where a lot of brothers and sisters just fight like cats and dogs all the time, all they have is arguments — it was a reasonably constructive relationship?"

"Mmm, yeah."

"So that could be what we're talking about?"

"That could be it, yeah."

"And his name is...?"

"Michael."

"Okay, so Michael's in there [indicating the past]. Was there another... I am trying to look beyond the family now... was there a relationship where distance was a problem?"

"Well, yes, in that I was away at school."

"Right, okay."

"So, geographically bound..."

"So there was that sort of geographical impediment to the wonderful flutterings of romance..."

[Nodding and plentiful agreement]

"That's another thing I see here, and I also think that relationship is behind you and it's past."

"Mmm." [agreement]

"Okay. Let's come forward a little bit more. I think that when you first got your first proper job, I think there was some kind of... it wasn't a very orthodox procedure. I think there was a big fluke involved... a slice of luck."

"Yes, possibly." [smiles]

"You say possibly, but I think it's making sense to you."

"Yes."

"Some people, they see the job advertised, they go for the interview, it's all very formal. I think there was some sort of marvellous fluke of luck that came your way."

"Mmm." [mild agreement]

"This means something to you."

"Mmm ." [mild agreement]

"Okay. It's not really contravening the sort of thing I spoke about earlier, where you're somebody who works hard for the things you get. But nonetheless..."

"Lucky, yes."

"Once or twice we all get dealt a good card, and there are elements here of skill but also of luck and fortune, particularly with regard to career. I spoke about an accident earlier... I don't see any major health worries that we can talk about in your child and teenage years."

"No."

"There wasn't anything like that."

"No." [shaking head]

"You've always enjoyed pretty good health and strength."

"Mmm." [agreement]

"Okay, that's fine.

I want to move on, because I'm aware that the [TV production] people want me to talk about the present and the future a little bit. But just more recently, and this is quite a fun one as well..."

"Is it?" [smiling / laughter]

"There are influences here, I'm talking about what we might call the festive season, Christmas and New Year, that sort of thing, there was some kind of... you haven't forgotten this and I think it's the sort of thing you probably talk to people about over a drink or over coffee. There was some kind of, er, something going wrong; some kind of 'Oh my God, why does this happen to me'. It could have been getting your dress snagged just as you were about to go out, or an appointment falling through or going to the wrong door..."

"Mmm..." [puzzled, cautious, only mild agreement]

"This is to do with a party or it could be around the festive season, Christmas, New Year, although that's just my first impression as to where people do their socialising. And I think it could be the end of last year, where there was some sort of social occasion where you were planning to meet, and there was some kind of terrible mess-up."

"Nothing terrible I can remember."

"No, okay, was there... is it just that I'm exaggerating too much. There was a sort of minor hiccup."

"Minor hiccup, I think."

"So it's not really as writ large as I was saying."

"No. I'm sorry!"

"Don't worry...! So, and was that to do with... and was it around the Christmas and New Year period though?"

"Yes. November-ish."

"Novemberish, okay, and that was something that directly affected you and also..."

"Well, yes, it was something that was easily resolved but I felt a bit stupid at the time."

"Well, easily resolved for *you*..."

[laughter and agreement]

"...but a lot of people could have been knocked sideways by it!

So let's just look back at that [referring to the reading so far]. There were some things that seemed to make sense there about your past life, and we found Michael in there. Maybe Michael will turn up again [gesture to the 'present' section of the layout]. Do you still see much of him? Because I feel distance there..."

"Yes, there is a distance and I haven't seen him since Christmas."

"Okay let's see what you're like now. This is usually the bit that people find [more interesting]. This is where you've been and this is where you are."

"And this is where we're going... yeah."

[assessing the cards] "Oh, well, I don't know if I want to sit here any more!" [light-hearted]

[laughs]

"Okay. No health problems, that's the first thing."

"No."

"You're quite a resilient, tough old boot, basically, if you don't mind me saying so. Let's talk about the fact that you're somebody who is educated but you'll never stop learning."

"Mmm." [agreement]

"You are somebody who is decisive and determined."

"Uh-huh." [agreement]

"There is actually a side of you which you keep very, very dark and nobody sees, and that is you can be hurt quite easily."

"Uh-huh." [agreement]

"And people don't realise this because they think you are quite strong on the outside, but between you and me and the cards, you actually are very sensitive. There are times over the past five or six years when you've been so hurt by things that people have done that they've actually changed your outlook."

"Mmm, probably..." [unsure]

"Okay, you say probably. I mean, I don't know, I'm not trying to be right or wrong. I'm just telling you the impressions I get. I have to comment here on a professional connection. I'm getting the impression of rendering a service to people that people enjoy, and of finance."

"Yes."

"Yes? Okay, I'm getting the impression that you handle numbers. You're numerate, and I don't think you have to do with stocks and shares because I don't think you're a gambler."

"Well, no."

"Okay, I get the impression that you have a professional image that you're working with people's finances... is this the right sort of area?"

"Yes."

"Okay, would it be right to say that you help them do something they can't do as well for themselves?"

"Yep."

"Okay, that's the sort of area that I see you working in."

[nodding and agreement]

"Okay. I don't believe you are married."

"Okay, no."

"No children."

"No."

"But one day you'd like to have children."

"Mmm... iffy!" [laughter]

"Iffy? Okay, it's not been decided. I think the concentration at the moment is very much on the career. Would it be right to say there's a possibility of yourself, deep down, wondering if the present job you're in is the right one for you?"

"Er, yeah." [surprised reaction]

"I think there is a connection here, a question in mind as to whether you might actually try your hand at something else or make a living at something else."

"Mmm." [very positive agreement]

"And that's to do with the creative ability which we saw over here."

"Yes."

"We've got The Popess here, let me just talk about this
[showing the card]. The Popess is a maternal figure, a feminine figure. She is a figure of the female strengths of perseverance and dedication and care and looking after the things that matter to you most. And I believe that there is a kind of protective custody around this creative ability that you have, which could be something like writing, but also could involve your sense of humour, your sense of creativity, your sense of fun. Is this something that you nurture, that you look after in yourself?"

"Yes."

"You'd agree with that?"

"Uh-huh." [agreement]

"Okay, and I think there's also..., your creativity is reactive as well as active. You have a responsiveness, you like music for example."

"Mmm." [agreement]

"Your music collection is pretty good."

"Mmm." [agreement].

"And you enjoy it and it's something that gives you quite a great deal of satisfaction."

"Mmm." [agreement].

"You're quite an outgoing person. I think anyone can see that, they don't need to look at the cards."

[laughter]

"But at the same time, would it be right [to say] you do a fair amount of the 'on the town' stuff?"

"Yeah."

"Clubs and this sort of thing?"

"Yeah, yeah."

"Maybe sometimes too much?" [light-hearted]

"You'll have to speak to my boss, but yes." [laughter]

"Okay. But he's not here so I have to ask you!" [shared laughter]

"Yep, yep."

"And you're aware of that, and I'm sure it doesn't get out of hand. There is a career option, not something that has been forced upon you. I don't think anybody has walked into your office recently and said you're going to be fired. I think that there is a creative aspect of you that isn't being fully sated at the moment in the job you do."

"Uh-huh." [agreement]

"Because the job you do is to do with numbers and finance and that sort of thing, is that right?"

"Yes."

"Okay, and I think there's an option open to you where you might be thinking well, I have a creative ability, I could try my hand. I don't think it's the visual arts it could be something like writing."

"Mmm." [agreement]

"And you could be thinking, well now, is that an option for me?"

"Is it viable?"

"Viable, yeah, okay, so there's something there that makes sense to you?"

"Uh-huh." [agreement]

"The other thing that I can see about you at the moment is that that's going to weigh very heavily on your mind. You are... you're going to laugh when I say this I'm sure..."

"Go on!"

"... you're not someone who is scrabbling around for money. You are comfortable."

"Yeah, I manage."

"You manage, and again part of that is something you would take credit for. It doesn't just happen."

"Yeah."

"Some people are careful with money and some people aren't. You are careful. You can be cautious. Your extrovertism doesn't actually manifest itself in the way that some sort of superficial reading might indicate. I don't think you're the sort who puts on a red nose and starts entertaining everyone at the drop of a hat."

"No, no."

"But nonetheless you're not going to be scared to give your opinion. You're not going to wait around just being the wallflower whilst everyone else tells the funny stories and anecdotes. You have a fair grasp of things, of life, geography and history. You can talk about various subjects, not just related to what you do for a living."

"Yeah."

"You have outside interests. You can talk about creative things, and writing, and music and this sort of thing."

"Mm-um." [plentiful agreement]

"You also have an interest in history?"

"Mmm... yes." [partial agreement]

"A mild one..."

"A mild one."

"... okay, but this again is nothing to do professionally. I think again at the moment there's something here about relationships. I think there's an option very close to you..."

"Mmm..." [partial agreement]

"...or in the very near future, where you have an option to say, well, something that's happening for you at the moment could take on a more permanent basis."

"Possibly, mmm."

"Yeah?"

"Okay."

"Okay. I mean, that's there, and we might have a look over here [the future] at what happens about that."

"Okay."

"And the other thing is that the kind of protectiveness that you've built around yourself over the years is going to be something which perhaps now and again, at the moment — and I say this just because I see it and I don't mean it too personally — it's something that you're going to have to shed a little bit of."

"Right."

"Because you could come across to people as a little bit too armour-plated, a little bit too cold. Is this something you recognise in yourself?"

"Yes."

"It is. Okay, well I see it here. When we get this many swords and things, it's very difficult to avoid it [picking up card]. King of Swords. And it might be quite nice if you were able to emphasise more of the feminine..."

"Girly?"

"Well, that's a slightly derogatory term, there are positive feminine attributes, or which are traditionally regarded as feminine traits! And I think you're also someone who is aware of politics but doesn't dwell on them too much."

"Yes."

"Because there's a lot of sense in you that politics is all the same and you always know what they're going to say so you can't really care much either way. Er, I'm just seeing correspondence of a financial nature which is going to affect..."

"What do you mean by correspondence?"

"Well, for example you could have recently been in touch with someone pursuing this option of whether your more creative side is viable or not."

"Yes."

"You've had a letter or some communication suggesting some input in that way."

"Yeah."

"That's one of the more recent things I see, but it's going on in the present."

[enthusiastic agreement]

"Okay, let's go over here [future]. I'm just going to turn over three, and then there's going to be three... what I'd like you to do is just nominate one of the last three. It's not a card trick or anything..."

"Pigeons won't fly out or anything? ...that one there."
[laughter]

"Okay that's the one we'll leave 'til last, because that's the decision card. Now then... Ace of Coins. Very good for financial..."

"Oh good!"

"...okay, let's just say that I don't think the next time Fortune compile their top 100 millionaires you're going to be on the list. But let's just say that the kind of financial good sense and management which is part of your life, and which you've shown all through your life... and which is something of a family trend, am I right?"

"Mm... yes." [partial agreement]

"Yeah OK. Grudgingly... that's fine."

[laughter]

"We can be wrong as well as right! This is going to develop and you'll have even more satisfaction in that regard. I don't really see you sitting under Waterloo in a cardboard box okay? *[Note: this used to be a London euphemism for being homeless]* So we've got coins. I think there is an option here definitely to... Page of Wands, Three of Wands... to take your own life in the direction that you want to."

"Right."

"I think there is an ability here to perhaps, er you may decide that the next big novel's going to have your name on it. Or something you've written for TV is going to have your name on it or something like this. There is a creative urge here which is going to come to fruition, I know that..."

"Successfully?"

"Well one of the things that the tarot refuses to do is deal in absolutes."

"Okay."

"Your version of success won't be the same as the next person's idea of success, so what do we consider successful?"

"Yeah..." [nodding in agreement]

"To some people it's just measured in pound signs, to some people ... even if nobody ever sees what they've written..."

"Sure, that they've actually done it..."

"...that they've done it, and to some people all you need is to show it one person and if that person enjoys it, well one person's enjoyed it."

"Right."

"So that's the kind of success. What I can see is that we have an ability here to take even more control of your own life than you already do. When we have this, the last of the Arcana cards, 21, The World, it tends to pertain to somebody who, as it were, creates her own dominion."

"Mm-um." [taking an interest in the card's meaning]

"And I think that you know that in the future one of the things you're going to do is, er, you will have even more things in your own life sorted out. You will be living where you want to live. You will have around you the things and the people that you want to have around you. I don't see you ending up in the sort of blind alley that, sadly..."

"... some people do."

"...some people do, let's admit it. And I think, there's the sort of people you have a coffee with them and all they do is moan about how everything's wrong in their lives. This isn't Susie. This isn't you."

"Right."

"Now, as I say, I think health is always going to be good for you, no matter how often you come and see me or somebody else..."

"Yep."

"...I don't think we're going to be talking about horrible things happening."

"Uh-huh." [agreeing this is unlikely]

"Although there could be throat area problems that might have afflicted you in the past. You know, you could be one of the first people who goes down with a sore throat when the bug's going round."

"Yeah."

"I don't know if that means anything to you... but it's that mild sort of thing."

"Right." [disinterested, but not disagreeing]

"Romance-wise... I see a lot more for you than perhaps you see for yourself."

"Oh, right! Okay!"

"There is a scope here to apply the same kind of determination and decision-making..."

"Yeah."

"...to somebody and say, you know, he might not know it at all but there's going to be a very productive partnership here."

"Right."

"More than just a business relationship, okay. And that will probably be somebody that you meet with regard to this creative side of your life and impulses."

"Right."

"Okay, you have actually asked me one direct question, which is about the success of your creativity. [Consulting the last card] Ah, this is where it would have been nice, for the sake of everything here, if I could have come up with some nice big resolution. We have the Six of Wands so let me talk about this card. What I can tell you is this, you're going to have to judge on your own terms what success means. I think perhaps it could be that you don't perhaps write the next John Le Carré, six is so sort of in the middle, you know the values."

"Average."

"Well, average in some ways. You see wands are to do with people who use their own creativity and their own power and their own ability to do things. What I suppose the tarot is suggesting here is that Susie is going to go ahead and do what she wants to do, and that in itself is going to give you a great deal of satisfaction. But if you're going to go into it just for the money, forget it."

"Yep."

"There has to be another motivation, there has to be something deeper to you, and I think you realise this yourself in your own core."

"Yes." [nodding].

"And that will be how you regard your own success. Hey, I mean if cheques start coming through the door, great!"

"Fine."

"If they don't, well you're not going to say, well that was the only way I was going to accept it. And I think that's the sort of answer that we're getting."

"Right."

"And we've had a look at where you've been, and where you are, and where you're going. And unless there's anything specific we want to go into, I'm quite happy to say I've done my best for you, and I hope that some of it made sense for you."

"Okay, lovely, thank you."

"And I think they want you to go and have a talk with somebody."

"Thank you and bye bye."

- - -

This concluded the reading. At the time, I had no idea what Susie made of it all or what she would say. For all I knew, she could have been ready to loudly denounce me as an obvious fake.

What the client said

After the reading, Susie was interviewed by the show's presenter, Sandi Toksvig.

- - -

Sandi: "Ian was wary because of all the lights and so on, it's not how he would normally do it. So was it all right?"

Susie: "It was fine. You know, not quite as scary as, you know, some people imagine or portray them to be. Yes, it was fine."

"So what sort of things were in the reading?"

"It went from past, present, future... I suppose one thing that went throughout was you're going to be reasonably solvent and reasonably healthy, which is fine, quite pleasant; that yes, maybe there's a creative bent, talent if you like, that hasn't been fulfilled and, you know, should you maybe jump to the other side and say 'bugger it, I'm going to do it' and worry about whatever else happens. But yes, it was reasonably happy, nice number of friends, quite outgoing. I mean there wasn't anything ominous. Whether he'd been asked not to say anything unpleasant, I don't know."

"I mean, were you surprised about how much he was able to gain about you?"

"Yes, it was not terribly... I mean there were quite a lot of specifics there, you know it's not like saying every Capricorn is this or whatever, yes I was."

"What were the specifics that particularly surprised you?"

"Well, I think the creative side, which people wouldn't necessarily know. I think maybe the solvency side, the connection with being quite close to my brother, that sort of thing."

"So over all, did you feel it was basically a good..."

"Yes, I mean I've never had one before so, you know, I've got nothing to compare it with. But I was reasonably impressed."

"I want to be absolutely clear, Susie, that until the reading you had never met Ian Rowland."

"I'd never met him, I'd never done any of this before."

"All right, now he come up with some fairly specific things: the name of your brother, the fact that you had an accident when you were young, the Christmas incident. Did that sort of give you a start, that he was able to do that?"

"Yes, it did. I think the brother, and the Christmas thing, yes. You know I came to it with an open mind, and you always think maybe these things are set up. But no, I'd never met him before. But yes, I mean it was quite surprising, because obviously he only chose two names and it was one of those."

"And were you trying, as it were, not to give anything away about yourself?"

"Well yes, I mean I answered questions. I didn't, you know, say anything."

"So what was your over all feeling about it?"

"I was quite impressed. In some ways now you've done it once you think, gosh, maybe there are people out there who know things about you that you may or may not want them to. But yes, I felt reasonably calm and happy about it."

"But surprised?"

"Yes, pleasantly."

- - -

In a separate part of the show, Susie was asked if she thought it possible I might have been some sort of fake or fraud. She said she did not think this was possible.

Review

This demonstration was one of the first I ever gave for TV. I do not regard it as a particularly strong example of cold reading in action. It is clear that I made a number of significant mistakes, such as failing to use what I earlier referred to as the Cream Principle: make weak statements first and then strengthen them if appropriate. There were too many occasions when I offered a strong statement first and then had to dilute it to fit.

Susie was also a little more astute than many typical clients. As her interview made clear, she realised that I had asked quite a lot of questions (most clients remain relatively unaware of this if the questioning is done well). However, Susie also claimed, rather confusingly, that she had given me very little information. In fact, she had given me ample feedback throughout, both verbal and non-verbal.

I am not trying to suggest this particular demonstration was a spectacular triumph. Nonetheless, Susie *did* come away feeling that I was genuine, and that there was something to tarot reading after all. She was genuinely impressed by what she viewed as my ability to identify specific details about her life, including things that *even* her friends did not know about.

The reading lasted 24½ minutes. In this time, I talked to Susie about:

- her personality, temperament, character, skills and talents
- incidents and relationships in her distant past
- incidents in the more recent past, and the present
- a current relationship
- her family, including the name of her brother
- her creative writing ability (which her friends did not know about)
- her career
- her hobbies and interests,
- her aspirations and ambitions, both personal and professional
- her feelings about herself, her career and her choices
- her finances
- her social life and social skills

These topics were covered with more or less total agreement the whole way. There were some times when Susie only partially agreed with my statements, but there was not a single occasion when she declared me to be wrong. This is not bad for nearly 25 minutes talking to a complete stranger!

Example 2: Prepared astrological reading

Introduction

This second example is taken from a documentary series called 'Heart of the Matter', made by Roger Bolton Productions for BBC Television. For this demonstration, I was asked to pose as an astrologer and to give the *same* astrological reading to two completely *different* clients. I agreed to prepare the reading in advance, and then to present it to the two clients in turn.

The story of this particular reading is quite interesting. I was quite busy with other projects at the time and as a result I left my preparation to the last minute. The evening before I was due to give the reading, at around midnight, I sat down at my computer and simply made up a reading that I felt sounded suitably astrological. I wrote it in more or less one go, with very little revision. By the time I had finished, I'd written about 3900 words.

I was not told the date of birth of either client or anything else about them. All I was told was that one was Virgo and the other was Taurus. When I wrote the reading I referred to Virgo throughout. I then used the word-processor to prepare a second version in which every reference to 'Virgo' was replaced with 'Taurus'. Otherwise, the two versions were identical.

To the best of my knowledge, not a single word of the reading bore any relation to genuine astrological theory or practice. I made up phrases like 'Sign of Virgo with Saturn rising' without the faintest idea what this is supposed to mean, or whether it actually applied to either client's horoscope. I merely wanted to add some astrological jargon to my made-up reading.

I also got some blank astrological charts, as used by astrologers, and drew interesting geometrical shapes, squiggles and signs on them as if these meant something.

The next afternoon, the taping went ahead as planned in a comfortable flat belonging to one of the production crew. I met the clients one at a time, and took them through the prepared reading. While it was possible for me to emphasise some sections of the reading more than others, the rules meant that I was not allowed to make any changes to either version, and both women were presented with the complete reading in its entirety.

I will have more to say about this reading in the 'Review'.

The clients

The first client (Virgo) was a very likeable, gently-spoken woman, in her late forties or early fifties, with a trace of a South African accent. She was pleasantly plump rather than athletic, and dressed for comfort rather than style. After the reading, it later transpired that she was married and had a modest interest in astrology.

The second client (Taurus) was a rather more confident young woman in her early twenties, and English. She was extremely slim and athletic, and her looks, make-up and stylish outfit made it clear she took great care over her appearance. Though polite and good-natured, she was clearly more noncommittal than the first. After I had completed the reading, it turned out that she was single, although in a long-term relationship, and was mildly sceptical about astrology.

I think you will agree these were very dissimilar women. All the more interesting, then, to see how they would react to the same identical reading.

The reading

Here is the Virgo version of the reading. The second was identical, but with the word 'Virgo' changed to 'Taurus' throughout.

- - -

Zodiac summary:

Sign of Virgo with Saturn rising

Principal planets:

First house: Venus, Neptune.
Fifth house: Mars.
Sixth house: Pluto.

Principal aspects:

Venus in Aquarius.
Neptune and Mars in Pisces.
Pluto in Sagittarius.

(1) The Virgo female

Affairs of the heart

The Virgo female is feminine, warm and loving, no stranger to strong passions and deep feelings. She is not as easily hurt as some, like her frailer friends Pisces or Gemini for example, but this resilience has a drawback. Since you are accustomed to feeling strong, and can take on the chin some knocks that would send others down for the count, you react all the more intensely when, as must sometimes happen, someone does manage to hurt or wound you. When this happens, you are stunned, amazed that your defences failed you. Moreover, you can be very effective at making your distress known to all around you.

You genuinely find it hard to give up your independence, indeed your every instinct challenges this very notion. You prefer to strike a well-managed balance between solo activities and those in tandem with your partner, to the benefit of both.

You do not bear grudges much. It's too time-consuming for you, and you prefer to simply move on and leave small nuisances behind. Those who cross you or treat you badly will most likely receive a sharp blast of icy contempt — one of your strong suits when the mood strikes — and then be left watching your heels through dust.

You can take a knock to your own pride or confidence, because you trust yourself to recover. But woe betide anyone who hurts or damages those whom you care for. You are a protector and a carer. You never, ever forget an enemy whom you perceive to have injured someone close to you. Nor do you forgive yourself for having allowed your protective skills to have been thwarted.

Incidentally, one such victory is all that any opponent can hope for. Should there ever be a return match, the female Virgo will prove herself a most fearsome adversary: well-prepared, serenely defiant, and, when joining for battle, resolutely invincible. Those who on the first occasion manage a successful attack would be wise upon a second meeting to reach for a white flag of surrender. Virgos do not take prisoners.

Career and self-advancement

The Virgo female can acquit herself well in most departments. She can be a great cook, a great businesswoman, a great artist or a great mother. Creativity is a strong point, and is likely to manifest itself in more than one form. She can write the great novel, or create a prize-winning garden. She can think and express herself visually, or learn to be a good dancer. Then again, her creativity can express itself in more subtle ways: in the way she talks, in the way she conducts her friendships and relationships, in her choice of gifts and presents, or in her ideas for holidays and other special occasions.

There are two problems that disturb this somewhat calm picture. First, you have a degree of inertia that may prevent you from exploring all the options before deciding which creative mode is right for you. This inertia is not physical or geographical. You may be a great traveller or the sort to move every two years. It is an inner inertia whereby you so enjoy the outlet you have discovered already that you overlook the possibility of there being something even better just around the corner.

The other problem is that you do not lack energy. Even if you are not inclined to be particularly athletic, you nonetheless find yourself possessed of enormous reserves of both creative and physical stamina. From this point of view, you may find it hard to find a role that can soak up all your capacity, and genuinely cater for your potential. This places you at a disadvantage compared to the more easily contented Aquarius, for example, or the less ambitious Libra. On the positive side, once you do find the right role, you can be relied upon to make the most of it, and leave the other contenders behind. A Virgo who has found something to excel at is a joy to herself and to others — always provided, of course, that they are not so foolish as to try and stand in her way.

(2) The story of the major houses

First house

Your first house is associated with affairs closest to the heart and to romance. Here, the influence of Venus, the guider of passion, is a very positive sign that you can succeed in love where many fail, although this is not to say you won't need some of your Virgo toughness, persistence and self-confidence from time to time.

The presence in this first house of Neptune, associated with deep-seated wisdom and a tempered approach to life's turbulence, augurs well for you. Though your life may pass through many phases, and love present its thorns as well as its roses, you have enough deep-seated faith in yourself to see you through and achieve the happiness and love that is your birthright, and for which you have more than average capacity.

Fifth house

Your fifth house is associated with career, self-advancement and personal wealth, although the stars do not see wealth in purely financial terms. The presence of Mars, the planet of energy, power and conquest, allied to your natural Virgo strength and fortitude, indicates that you have an enviable capacity to work hard for what you want, and to overcome any obstacle that might defeat a less determined character.

However, you can only bring these formidable strengths to bear once you have truly committed yourself to a chosen line or path, and this is where you may come unstuck. Your innate tendency is to stick to the tried and true, to stay comfortable where you are, and to settle for what you've got. In other words, your ability to forge ahead, determine new horizons and achieve any or all ambitions, may go untapped as you decide to take the easier, quieter life. It would be a shame to squander this power and potential for conquering new challenges.

Sixth house

Your sixth house is associated with learning, intellect and communication. Your primary influence here is Pluto, the planet of peace, contemplation and solitude. This would suggest someone who is never ending in her search for new understandings, new perspectives and new ways of seeing the world. You are already aware of how much you have learned in life, and of the things now clear that once frustrated and puzzled you. You are a voyager and a traveller, who has gained much in experience and who has learned to trust to this experience when a challenge presents itself, or life takes a turn for the worse.

Virgos do not generally aspire to abstract intellectual goals that may have little pragmatic value. They enjoy learning, so long as they see a tangible benefit and a practical improvement in their quality of life. Pluto will moderate your natural tendency to confront problems head on, and encourage you to adopt more subtle and creative strategies. You prefer to outwit the problem instead of charging at it. This makes for a very effective combination, and you should be a good learner and thinker; someone whom friends know can usually be relied upon to solve a problem using either sheer will and determination, or a smart-ish piece of lateral thinking which others would have missed.

(3) Who you are: your zodiac traits

The communicator

You are a communicator. In the past five years you have discovered fresh talents in this direction, happy to share with others the benefit of your knowledge and experience. You are not some chattering busy-body. The advice you give, and the suggestions you make, are always firmly grounded in reality and 100% practical. You can think through the practicalities of any situation, and rarely let small problems get in your way. Your friends see you as helpful, a good ally in a tight corner, and welcome your strength.

If there is a drawback here, it is that now and again you don't really know when to stop. Inwardly, you know that others have to lead their own lives, but you can't help feeling you have enough imagination for two, as indeed you do, and are plagued by nagging suspicions that if only they would just leave everything up to you, you would get further, faster, and with less fuss.

The achiever

The flustered, hysterical approach is totally alien to you. Calm, methodical, planned — these are your hallmarks. Only the most serious frustrations, arising from almost unbelievable bad luck can unsettle you and at such times all around would be well-advised to steer clear. A female Virgo sensing that she has lost control is not an attractive sight, and needs extremely careful handling. She will calm down when she's good and ready, and when she does there will be a full-throttle display of short, sharp action designed to put her house back in order and restore the sense of security that is so precious to her. It would be most unwise for anyone to try and intervene or to obstruct this process.

The participant

You are a doer, not a fantasist; a performer not a critic; a participant rather than an observer. Quiet contemplation, despite the influence of the lofty Pluto, is not your scene. Get involved, get with it, get in on the action — this is you. On occasions you go too far: you want to run the whole show, overlooking that others also want to make their contribution. However, provided you manage to check this tendency, you are a valued team player and one with enormous heart.

Your deep-rooted pride will simply not allow you to let the side down. Whatever role you accept, you always play it to the full. This is not just admirable selflessness on your part: your powerful sense of independence is ever with you, and underneath whatever mask you may wear, you want your share of the limelight, your share of the praise. But if you rather obviously crave some of the rewards, at least you are prepared to work hard to obtain them, and others can see this in you.

The schemer

If you were to be totally candid, you would have to admit that although your first choice is to win fair and square, you are not beyond stretching an ethical point in your favour in exceptional circumstances. If you sense the game is a little bit rigged against your interests, and the fair approach simply won't work, then you can quickly decide that the ends justify the means, and to take whatever route you have to in order to win. You are honest, and even your worst enemy could not say you aren't, but you're not a saint and frankly you've never felt fluttering wings and a harp were really your style.

163

(4) Trends of the recent past and present

Romance

The past five years have seen at least one major romantic line that became a tangled knot, and ultimately left you somewhat cynical in your outlook. You recovered, as you always do, but not by chirpily 'bouncing back' and pretending all is well. This is not your style. You did it by carefully assessing what you had learned from the experience, and promising yourself that you will be more circumspect in the future. Problems could arise if you have now gone too far the other way and are too cautious in forming new friendships, associations and relationships.

Always remember that Venus is one of your first house planets, and her strong romantic influences are not easily subdued, nor should they be. You can be a terrific lover: understanding, fiercely loyal, playful, committed, able to think for two and, when the needs arise, be the one who provides the strength and the determination that can see both you and your partner through difficult times. Nor is it hard for you to receive love. You frankly relish attention and affection, and are willing to earn both in abundance. Your relationships would never fail for want of stability or of effort. You have both in spades.

Where you are vulnerable is in being perhaps too strong for some partners, who find your boundless inner fortitude and spirit rather too much to handle. Also, you sometimes opt for personal comfort and contentment rather than the challenge of a new relationship, or a new phase in an existing one. In this regard, you do sometimes show the lack of influence from dynamic Mercury or Saturn, the great promoter of initiative and planning.

Learning and new experience

Over the past five years, you have exercised your great capacity for new learning, and for acquiring what one could describe in the broadest sense as new wisdom. There is a conflict here. The planetary aspect of Pluto inclines you towards wisdom for its own sake, like a scholar in an ivory tower. Yet as a Virgo, you feel inclined to make the effort to learn only when you can see a practical, material benefit at the end.

This inner conflict has manifested itself over the past five years. On the one hand, with Pluto's influence, you are the dabbler, readily dipping into everything under the sun, something of an intellectual scavenger. You don't care where you find information (books, pictures, conversation) or how it might help you in your goals. You value it for its own sake, and tell yourself you never know when it might come in handy. You make a great conversationalist, provided you find someone of similar temperament.

On the other hand, being Virgo, you find yourself inclined to harbour your resources to the full, and not waste any precious time or energy in pursuit of new learning if you can't see the point, the practical benefit. This is a conflict you will find hard to resolve, and yet resolve it you must if you are to realise your potential. The Martian aspect of your fifth house suggests that your Virgo side will win the day. You will become better at focusing your reserves on one or two carefully chosen goals, and then working towards them with your characteristic determination and resourcefulness. This process may already have begun, but it is almost certainly not yet complete.

It would be unfortunate for anyone to try and stand in between you and your chosen goal. They will not find it at all a comfortable place to be. If they are wise, they will stand aside, or perhaps help you and ally themselves to your formidable strength. If they are not so wise, they may try to oppose you or divert you from your chosen course. Their chances of success are slim. The sheer strength of your Virgo nature, welded to the strong presence of the warrior Mars, is a powerful combination and not one to be tackled lightly. An opponent's only real hope is that you will give up, or simply cease to apply yourself to your goal. This sometime happens when Virgos find themselves in a nice spot some part way along their journey, and opt for a bask in the sunshine rather than making further progress.

Money and finance

Your chart does not suggest that you lack for the material pleasures that mean the most to you. You have financial concerns, and it is probably correct to say that some financial stress will always be with you. You are neither governed by money nor a slave to it. The truth is that despite your admitted materialistic streak, you simply do not consider money important enough for your life to revolve around its management and accumulation. Pluto, in your sixth house, would never allow you to get so interested in such mundane affairs. Hence over the past five years you have managed to make a little money grow, but you have also witnessed your ability to wave goodbye to it, enjoy the proceeds and let tomorrow take care of itself.

As a Virgo, your principal concern is for the comforts of the present, and the needs of the now. You are not unconcerned about the future, but it takes second place in your heart to the pleasures and satisfactions that you can enjoy now. 'A bird in the hand is worth two in the bush' could almost be your motto. In this regard, you will always be at odds with Cancer, the typical long-distance planner if ever there was one, and Capricorn, whose fastidious attention to tiny details would leave you cold.

Health

There are no major oppositions in your chart that would indicate serious health problems or risks in adult life, although when you were younger, before your had matured into your natural strength and resilience, there may have been more than one serious cause for worry. For now, you are careful enough to take care of yourself where and when it matters.

Many Virgos do make fine athletes, but they tend to do so by dogged persistence and determined training, allied to a fierce drive to be first, rather than natural athletic grace or gifted reflexes. Hence you are unlikely to be the fitness freak among your circle, and not one to revolve your life around the local gymnasium. If these activities interest you at all, it is purely as a pragmatic means to an end — to feel better about yourself, to please yourself or your partner, or to prove something to yourself.

The strong influence of Mars in your fifth house suggests that whatever routine health problems you face you will see through with characteristic resilience and inner steel. You are not the sort to buckle easily under life's stresses and strains. Hypochondria is not to your taste. Whenever life fights you, you fight back, and you win far more often than you lose.

(5) Trends for the future

Mars moving into Pisces this year. Sagittarius moving into your fifth house this year. Pluto gaining ascendance from next spring. Mars waning from the following winter.

Success and ambition

Your are not one to trust to fate, to sit back and see how things turn out. You rightly feel yourself to be the architect of your own future, and you have a healthy sense of responsibility for your own actions.

The good things in life are yours for the taking. Not without effort. Not without challenge. Not without hardship. But you must not let these factors deter you. Remember, you have more than enough skills and talents at your disposal to see yourself through, and when all else fails your sheer force of will is going to see you through. You are a realist, and you know that everything in life comes at a price. Keep your realistic outlook, and you will not go far wrong.

Those ambitions closest to your heart now are ones that you have harboured over the past 18 months at least (ever since Neptune's ascendance in your first house became the dominant conjunction). If you can marshal your reserves correctly, and reign in the occasional flashes of temper that can cost you so dearly, then you will see your goals achieved.

Despite your occasional daydream of celebrity and exalted attention (all Virgos crave a touch of the 'star for a day' treatment) great fame and fortune is not indicated and wouldn't suit you anyway. What is indicated is something altogether more satisfying. You will reap the benefits of your more methodical, well-paced progress through life. While some of your contemporaries, the early meteors who blazed a brighter trail, are seen to burn out, you will be coming into your prime and enjoying the treasures you have patiently laid up for yourself.

You will never lose your taste for comfort, and luckily for you the experience of luxury will become more frequent with the passing of time.

Love

Few Virgos are ever truly unhappy in love. Even during spells of relative solitude, they can find contentment and much to enjoy in life. Your path is one favourable to strong and lasting love. Yes, you will continue to be too cautious and careful where romance is concerned. Yes, you will continue to squander some of the affection and warmth that could be yours by being a little too strong, and perhaps stubborn, for some people. But in spite of all, you have such warmth to offer, and make such a steadfast, supportive partner, that you can hardly fail to enjoy the well-founded relationships that are your birthright.

Attachments at their strongest now will remain so for the next year at least, although the passionate influence of Mars is due to wane a little from next year onwards. New attachments are indicated whether you want them or not, but yours will be the controlling hand that decides exactly how close a new presence is allowed to get. You are not to be trifled with, and people do not take long to realise this about you. Problems will only arise if you start to shirk this power, to worry about exploiting your formidable strength of character. With both Venus and Mars as powerful influences at birth, albeit in different houses, you cannot contentedly be one of life's shrinking violets. Yours is the active, determining role. A relationship *you* want to happen *will* happen. A relationship *you* want to be stronger *will* be stronger.

Know that this is so, and enjoy the consequences! Yours is one of the most sensual signs of all, and few can extract more enduring happiness, romance, passion and companionship from a well-founded relationship than the Virgo female.

Health

In general, good news. You have many untroubled years ahead when your faculties, both physical and mental, will serve you well in pursuit of your ambitions. You are naturally disposed to take an interest in your health, and are rarely if ever inclined to be reckless in health matters or to take unnecessary risks.

Keep your sense of prudence where health is concerned. It has served you well so far, and will continue to do so.

There is one warning sign. You cannot realistically expect to always enjoy the same strength and stamina as you do now. Taking the long-term view, the danger lies in not accepting this natural process of gradation and change, and one day imposing too great a strain on yourself through failing to acknowledge the passing of the years. Beware your innate obstinacy and pride in these matters. There is no shame in making suitable adjustments to your life to reflect each change in station.

This is a long-term concern. You are in no way past your peak, and have many years ahead when you can still enjoy your natural vigour. But when the time comes to ease off a little, do not resist or resent this process.

- - -

This concludes the text of my prepared pseudo-astrological reading. Remember, this exact same reading was given to both clients. The only difference was that in the second version I replaced 'Virgo' with 'Taurus' all the way through.

What the clients said

After each reading, the client was interviewed by the show's presenter, Joan Bakewell. The first client's interview was as follows.

- - -

Joan: "Okay, well Bridget, you've had your reading, your horoscope. How do you react to it? What do you make of it?"

Bridget (Virgo): "On reflection I suppose I have to think a lot of it, take the bits which he read me which I... and put them to use as to how I want to do them. It was more involved a reading to what I've perhaps had before, in that I expected him to say 'you should be a writer, you have a domineering personality'. Whereas he didn't. He intimated what he thought I was rather than saying exactly... which is better in a way... mind you, as he did point out at one point that you go off and become that person or that thing, because that's what you've been told."

"But did he get you right?"

"Yes I would say 99.9% of it was right. Mind you, I thought he would bring in other bits which are renowned Virgos, but then again I suppose that's the newspaper tabloid part of a Virgo, you know, the regular star magazine."

"So what did he get right about you?"

"He said that I'm precise and that once I start something I go at it. He said something about a romantic intimation that I had changed in the last five years or something. I need to read that a bit more deeply. But I think obviously then I must put it to what I think. I wasn't involved with somebody in the last five years but my relationship changed greatly with my husband, and all I can assume is that that's what it means. But you have to put them into something that you think is going to suit the way you feel about it."

"And what about the future? Did you get any clues as to that?"

"No, he said there was going to be a change in the next 6 months, what started 18 months, 6 months ago... something about I have to now finish off something that I thought I've always wanted to. Clean things up and get on to what I want to do."

"Does that ring a bell?"

"Yes in a way it does I suppose. I write bits here and there and I thought to myself, well, perhaps he means I really have to start that book now, you know. There's a book in all of us isn't there? And I think maybe I have to do it now."

"Do the things he's told you... they are going to change how you behave, a little?"

"No, I would say I don't really think so, no."

"But about this book?"

"Well yes, I mean he's just making... how do you put it ... clarifying perhaps what I've been thinking. Yes, in that way maybe you're right. Whether I'm going to sit down when it gets to six months and say my god, six months is here I really should have started this book because, you know, I was told that things were going to be done in 6 months, it might be in the 7th or 8th. I'm not saying that because he said it I will do it in that amount of time."

"Nevertheless what he's told you has been helpful to you?"

"Yes, sure, character-wise I suppose, yes."

"Do you follow your stars?"

"Yes I do, in the newspapers. Don't we all? Don't we all like to know we're going to meet a tall dark stranger, handsome man somewhere?"

"I mean you follow it daily, or slavishly, or just out of interest...?"

"I think actually we read them daily, my husband and I both do. Whether we put any reference to it I don't know. I think you just put it down to what happened today and what's going to happen tomorrow. One of the interesting things he said was about health. He said I had a good health, but that I think... one way he put it was something about I don't accept... you know, how as you get a bit older you can't do the things you did 5 or 10 years ago. And he's absolutely right when he says that I have to learn to accept that gracefully and tone down what your abilities are with your ageing. Otherwise my health was good. Which was encouraging to know, because I do tend to get really frustrated just 'cos I can't open a bottle I used to be able to open a year ago."

"And was he clear in the exposition he gave you? Did it seem clear?"

"Mm, I can't really say. Only the bits I heard that I wanted to take in at that particular time. Yes, I suppose so. I suppose it's something you need to do on a much... read into much more, then to be able to decide yes it was."

"Has it made you feel better, Bridget?"

"I suppose so. I suppose in a way where you can take it away and think about it and reflect on it and think well yes, I'm going to. Perhaps made me a bit more positive. (laughs) Is that good?"

- - -

This concludes the first interview.

Here is the second client's interview.

- - -

Joan: "Laura, what was it like as an experience?"

Laura (Taurus): "Very interesting. I was very impressed. I do go into these things very sceptical, and I wait for them to prove to me what they think I'm like and only then will I come round to that. So yes, he was very good."

"And did he prove it?"

"Yes. Yes, definitely."

"What did he get right?"

"Nearly everything. Really, nearly everything. I got flashbacks of when I was younger, that I could put points that he told me to. The only thing he probably wasn't right was the... sort of, love aspect at the moment. 'Cos I'm in a longstanding relationship which is rock-solid, it has been the whole way through. Again, he picked up with new boyfriends and things like that which hasn't happened."

"Thought there might have been a hiccup two years ago?"

"No, no, nothing there at all."

"Now what about being a schemer?"

"Definitely, I'm definitely a schemer, yep. I cheat at games. I will go out of my way to make sure I win things. Definitely. At the back of my mind I'll be scheming to get my own way."

"Were you surprised he discovered that?"

"Yes. Yes, very much so."

"Because there were no clues."

"No. Not at all. I don't know whether that's a Taurean trait, or me as a person but yes I'm definitely a schemer."

"Will what he's told you change your attitude to things?"

"The health problem bothered me a little bit because yes, I'm definitely like that. I will plough on because I'm very strong and I will just go hundred miles an hour on everything I do, which I do, and I can't see myself slowing down when I get older. So that I'll probably take on board and see what I can do about that in the future."

"So you would let it affect your behaviour?"

"Yes, yes definitely."

"What do you think of the person he presented. The true you?"

"Yes, mmm definitely."

"How much didn't match, how much did match?"

"I would say 95% of it matched. There were a few points probably he wasn't so on the nail, but it was very minimal, so I totally took on board everything he said."

"What do you make of the whole technique?"

"It's very interesting. To be honest I wouldn't have believed it. I can't see how anybody could predict exactly what a person's like from the time and date you were born. But, he proved me wrong!"

"You're impressed?"

"Yes, definitely."

- - -

At a later date, for another section of the same documentary, both women were interviewed again. They were asked if they thought there was any chance *at all* that I was some sort of con artist, rather than a genuine astrologer. Both women declared that they did *not* think this was possible.

Review

I always enjoy taking part in TV shows, but I recall this occasion as being especially happy and enjoyable. I would like to place on record my thanks to all concerned. The production team did an excellent job of organising the whole experiment, and they enforced all the conditions very strictly. I was naturally very pleased to hear that my reading was considered to be "99.9%" and "95%" accurate! It was also most intriguing to hear the more sceptical of the two clients suggest I had 'proved' that astrology works.

Same reading, second use

Some time after the above demonstration, I was contacted by British journalist, broadcaster and author John Diamond. John was writing a piece on psychics for 'She' magazine. He had already seen three professional psychics, and for comparison he wanted me to give him the cold reading treatment (even though he knew I was a fake). Being pushed for time, I simply rehashed the above reading on the computer so that the sign was 'Taurus' and the gender was changed from female to male throughout. Otherwise, I left it exactly as it was. I duly presented the reading to John, and his considered judgement was that it was "about 88%" accurate. This was a higher rating than he gave to any of the three psychics he consulted!

[At this point I must digress briefly. In 1997, after the above meeting, John Diamond was diagnosed with cancer. He eventually passed away in March 2001. John wrote a truly wonderful book called 'C: Because Cowards Get Cancer Too', about his experiences from the initial diagnosis onwards. There are simply no words to describe how excellent this book is or how rewarding it is to read. Incredibly moving and often very funny, yet never morbid or self-pitying, it is superbly well-written and I suggest that you read it.]

Same reading, third use

On another occasion, I was invited by Paramount Television to be a guest on the 'Leeza Gibbons' show in Los Angeles. They too wanted a cold reading demonstration, but the set up was a little different. They arranged things so that before the show I met four women from the studio audience for five minutes each. This time I posed as a clairvoyant. I had neither tarot cards nor an astrology chart. All I had were my 'psychic vibrations'.

As I met each client, I told her that once I had picked up whatever I 'sensed' about them, I would prepare a report that the production team would quickly type up and present for her assessment. This was untrue. Before flying to LA, I simply re-vamped the above reading, deleting the astrological jargon and replacing it with terms more suited to a clairvoyant reading. Otherwise, I left it unchanged. I printed out four identical copies and took them with me on the plane. These were the 'reports' that the four 'Leeza' audience members received. All four of them gave it a better than 80% accuracy rating!

I must mention in passing that this was another very enjoyable TV experience, and the producers did a wonderfully efficient job of setting up this experiment despite an acute lack of time. I was also made to feel very welcome by all concerned, which was nice given that I was four thousand miles from the damp little rock I call home.

All in all, the reading has served me very well indeed. Its basic content has been dressed as an astrological reading for a female Virgo, a female Taurean and a male Taurean. It has served as a clairvoyant report. It has been presented to intelligent 'clients' who ranged from the mildly credulous to the openly sceptical, from South Africa, England and America. It has always been rated as *at least* "80% accurate", and in its original form secured votes of "99.9%" and "95%" accuracy.

Progress Review

In Section Three, we have seen two examples of cold reading under test conditions. I believe these demonstrations are strong evidence that cold reading really works. Whether any psychics in real life actually use cold reading is a separate question, and one that I will leave to your judgement.

Having looked at how cold reading works, it is interesting to look at how to *prevent* it working. This is the subject of Section Four. Before that, a second and final Interlude.

Interlude: On Keeping An Open Mind

The notion of 'keeping an open mind' arises so often in the context of psychic readings that it warrants separate discussion. Time and time again, I have seen psychics urging commentators, clients, sceptics, TV viewers, journalists and anyone else who will listen to 'keep an open mind'. The implication is that an open mind is a characteristic of the fair, the reasonable and the intelligent. By implication, anyone who does *not* have an open mind is unfair and unreasonable, and hence their views can be dismissed. This is nonsense.

An open mind is appropriate in situations *where we have no good evidence one way or the other*. Suppose I meet someone for the first time. Should I be prejudiced about that person's character or integrity based on their looks or race or creed or accent or anything else? Of course not. I should retain an open mind as to what that person is like. They may turn out to be among the most fascinating, likeable and charismatic people I have ever met. Or not. Time will tell.

The same applies to other facets of life. If I want to pursue a given goal, perhaps creative or business-related, should I assume from the start that I will never succeed and my efforts will be wasted? Not at all. It is far better to retain an open-mind, to give it my best shot — with a positive attitude and the corresponding positive effort — and see where I get to.

What about those involved in scientific research? Should they be making pre-judgements about what they will, or will not, discover? Just to take one example, will research into genetic engineering ultimately provide a cure for cancer? An open mind is all we can have, because at the moment we just do not know.

In all these cases, an open mind is appropriate. However, it is inappropriate to keep an open mind in cases *where there is already plentiful evidence backing one view as against another*.

Imagine you are in a plane flying at 20,000 feet. The captain of the plane starts thinking along these lines, "Everything in the history of aeronautical science, and *every* experience of *every* airline pilot in history, suggests that to keep this thing in the air I need to keep the engines running. But hey, I'm going to keep an open mind. I'm going to cut all the engines, and dump our remaining fuel. Who knows, maybe the plane will still fly."

Do you really want that captain to keep an open mind about this?

Or imagine you're dining with friends at a favourite restaurant, and you have ordered the tomato soup. Do you really want the chef to be thinking, "Well now, *everything* we know about human nutrition, and *every* ounce of gastronomic training I have, suggests that I should *not* add a large dose of cyanide to this soup. But hey, I'm going to keep an open mind. Maybe it will taste better, and everyone will love it."

These are absurd examples, but only because the notion of keeping an open mind in these circumstances is absurd. It is similarly absurd with regard to the claims made by psychics.

Serious and devoted psychic research dates back to at least the start of the 20th century. It has been vigorously pursued all around the world, and in some cases has been extremely well-funded (often courtesy of military budgets in search of a new advantage over the enemy). This is a lot of research, in a lot of places, over a lot of time. All this work, all this effort and all this time has failed to deliver any good evidence *whatsoever* that psychic ability exists — at least, not of the kind allegedly manifesting itself in psychic readings.

This does not amount to *proof* that psychic beliefs are bogus remnants of outmoded, irrational and superstitious models of the world we live in. But it does amount to good reason to abandon an 'open mind', and to say instead that if the believers want us to acknowledge the reality of psychic ability, the onus is on them to prove their case. Whatever proof they provide, it will have to consist of something that cannot equally be attributed to the effectiveness of cold reading.

In cases where prior knowledge is available, the alternative to 'an open mind' is not 'a closed mind'. It is 'an informed mind'. In such contexts, any appeal to 'keep an open mind' is an appeal to prefer ignorance over knowledge. This is not advisable.

Section 4: Blocking Techniques

"Men become superstitious, not because they have too much imagination, but because they are not aware that they have any."

- George Santayana, 'Little Essays'

Five rules

Cold reading is a versatile process. It can be used to deliver any kind of psychic reading. What is more, it seems to work on virtually any client, no matter how intelligent or sceptical they are. In fact, there is literally only one way in which it can fail: if the client knows how cold reading works, and knows how to block it, then cold reading cannot succeed.

By reading this far, you have learned how cold reading works within the psychic context. In this section, I want to present you with five golden rules for blocking any attempt to use cold reading on you.

In case you want to try these rules out by actually going to a psychic, I need to make a point about recording the reading.

Recording the reading

These days many psychics offer to record the reading for you so that you can review the recording at your leisure. The problem is that if the psychic is recording the reading, she controls that recording. If she is unhappy with the way things have gone, she can and will refuse to hand it over. For example, if she has given up on the reading she may well make no charge (or refund your money) but at the same time refuse to give you the recording.

It is not in the psychic's interests to have this intriguing souvenir of her abject failure freely available. Who knows, you might want to play it to your friends or a local journalist. You may even feel inclined to put it on the internet somewhere.

For this reason, *you need to make your own recording.* You can do this covertly using a concealed microphone and recorder. Alternatively, you can openly place your own recording device on the table. The psychic may get rather wary and assure you that she is happy to record the session for you. All you need is some plausible reason why you prefer to do it yourself. Here are some ideas:

- you are something of an audio buff, and all your digital recordings use a special, high-quality file format (make something up) that you think gives best results

- you are a Capricorn and you are therefore fond of operating technical gadgetry

- you were given the recorder by your partner, and he/she will feel hurt if you do not use their lovely gift

- a long time ago a very good psychic told you always to record your own readings, as then they become more a part of your own spiritual life

With your knowledge of cold reading and your trusty recording device in operation, you are ready to block the cold reading process. Here are the five golden rules.

Stay reasonable

It is important for effective blocking that you keep perfectly calm, polite and good-natured at all times. This puts you in a position of control, and means you can think and act in a considered and effective manner.

It is also the fairest approach. If you were to adopt a hostile stance this would, according to psychic lore, block a totally genuine psychic attempting to give you the benefit of authentic psychic ability and insight. This is not the aim. The aim is to block cold reading being passed off as something else. So keep your cool, be pleasant, sweet and good-natured. Stay interested in the reading, and be grateful to the psychic for her time and effort.

Identify questions

The earlier section on 'Extracting Information' detailed many different ways in which cold readers can ask questions without making this obvious. Do not let the psychic get away with this. If you are asked a question, clarify that this is the case. You can say something like this:

"I'm sorry, but I'm confused. Are you telling me something, or are you asking me to give you information?"

This forces the central issue out into the open: are you receiving information or being asked to provide it? If the psychic uses information prompts such as, "Can you find a connection?", it is important to point out that the psychic is asking questions:

"Just let me understand this correctly. Are you now telling me something, or are you asking me to tell you something? Is that a question?"

This is important preparation for blocking technique number 3.

Do not answer questions

In a supposedly psychic reading you are paying to *receive* information, not to *provide* it. Hence whenever you are asked a question, or otherwise prompted for information, you are entitled to decline to offer information. There are many fair and polite ways of doing this. Here is one fairly direct approach:

> *"I'd prefer not to answer questions. I'm more interested in what you can tell me than what I can tell you. So please carry on with the reading. I'm sure it will be fascinating."*

A useful addition, if you need it, is to provide a rationale that is supportive of psychic ability, like this:

> *"I have some sceptical friends who like to think fake psychics just prompt their clients for information. I want to make sure I don't provide any information, so that I can assure my friends that your psychic abilities are genuine."*

When you get more direct prompts, such as ,"Tell me, who is Jane?", you can point out that the question is meaningless:

> *"I'm sorry, I don't understand the question. 'Who is Jane?' doesn't mean anything. Could you be a little clearer what you're getting at?"*

Another time-honoured blocking technique is simply to answer a question with a question. After all, if the psychic can ask questions, so can you! Continuing with the 'Who is Jane?' example, you could come back with:

> *"Which Jane do you mean?"*

Or:

> *"What's her surname?"*

Either of these responses are poisonous to the cold reading process, but perfectly fair for a genuine psychic. Why should the tarot be able to deliver first names but not surnames?

If the situation becomes argumentative, remain calm and unruffled and address the issue directly:

> *"I don't understand this. Are you saying that you are unable to give me a reading unless I give you information first? I feel that would be like me talking to a mirror. I'm having trouble understanding what's meant to be psychic about this."*

Do not provide feedback

As we have already seen, cold reading relies to a great extent on feedback. It follows that taking care not to provide any feedback tends to derail the cold reading process. One way to do this is to evade questions. Another way is to provide feedback that is useless for cold reading purposes. For example, suppose the psychic offers a response cue such as, "And I believe this is making sense to you isn't it?". You can say:

"I really don't know. I'd need time to think about what you're saying, and mull it over. You know, it's a bit difficult here and now to just agree or disagree right off the top of my head. I'll think about it later, when I have time to think it over properly."

There are countless variations on the same theme. You may like to review all the earlier sections that explained how psychics try to prompt clients for feedback. It is worth developing a repertoire of responses that are totally non-committal and uninformative yet encourage the psychic to carry on. Your bywords should be indecision, delay and ignorance. Here are some suggestions:

"I can't really decide if I agree or not. It's hard to say. I'll think about it. Please carry on, this is fascinating."

"I'm unsure on that. You may have something, you may not. I'll consider it later. What's next?"

"I wouldn't really know. I'd have to get back to you on that one. I'll certainly bear in mind what you're saying."

There are not many cold readers who could succeed in the face of this consistent lack of feedback.

Sabotage the elements

In Section Two of this book we saw 38 elements that can play a part in cold reading. Every single element has an underlying structure or formula. In every case, if you understand the formula, you can completely sabotage that particular element. You do this by (a) openly addressing the structure or formula involved, and then (b) subverting it.

Let us look at a few of the more common examples, starting with the Rainbow Ruse. The psychic offers something like this:

"You can be a very considerate person, but there are times when you recognise a selfish streak in yourself."

If you understand how the Rainbow Ruse works, you know that it credits the client with both a personality trait *and* its opposite, thereby covering all the bases. Hence the appropriate blocking technique is to bring out this structure, and ask for a description that says you are one thing or the other:

"I'm sorry, but what you've just said sounds as if you're telling me I am considerate but I'm also not considerate. I don't follow. Which one do you mean?"

In similar vein, consider a Greener Grass statement. If you happen to be evidently a very 'career-oriented' sort of person, you might get offered a Greener Grass statement about domestic and family life. You know that this kind of statement works by attributing to the client some hankering after the life choices she did not pursue. To block it, you bring out the structure and then defeat it, like this:

"Oh I see, you mean that I could be interested in the other choices that I might have made in life, but didn't. Well, I have to disagree. I'm happy with the choices I made. That's why I made them."

I am sure you are getting the hang of the idea. Next, let us try a Fuzzy Fact. Here is an example from the earlier section:

"I can see a connection with Europe, possibly the UK or it could be the warmer, Mediterranean part?"

The same blocking formula applies. First, you bring out the underlying structure (in this case, the complete lack of any meaningful context). Then, you render it useless. Like this:

"Well it's kind of hard for me to answer that until I know what you mean. What sort of connection are you talking about? Personal, social, professional... or what? Are you referring to the present or the past? And what do you mean by 'a connection' anyway?"

I could provide more examples but I feel I have laboured the point enough already. The basic blocking technique remains the same: bring out the structure, then blow it to pieces.

Bonus section: psychic baiting

When I wrote the first edition of this book, I included a section that I called 'Psychic baiting'. I felt it would be understood as an amusing, light-hearted section of the book that was not meant to be taken very seriously. Unfortunately, some people who work in the psychic industry did take it seriously and raised one or two objections.

In preparing the current edition, I did consider omitting this section altogether. In the end I decided to retain it because some readers have told me they enjoyed it. However, since it seems there is a risk of being misunderstood, let me make it clear: this is only a bit of fun and I am not seriously suggesting anyone should go around baiting psychics in the manner described.

For one thing I don't think it would serve any purpose, and for another it could lead to some rather angry and confrontational scenes. The world has quite enough of that sort of thing already and we don't need any more. I hope this is perfectly clear. All that having been clarified, here's a slightly revised and condensed version of the original 'Psychic Baiting' section.

Psychic Baiting is a fun way to pass your leisure hours. It's the only sure way to show that someone giving readings is using cold reading as opposed to genuine psychic ability. It involves going for a reading and allowing the psychic, which I stress means 'cold reader' in this case, to get snared by her own methods.

All that you have to do, as the client, is to wait until the psychic makes a statement that is *not* true. Given the prevailing standards of the contemporary psychic industry, you shouldn't have long to wait. You start the baiting process by agreeing with this erroneous statement as if it were true. You then encourage the psychic to develop this particular theme while you add even more disinformation. Finally, you confess your surprise that she can 'see' so many things that either aren't true or don't exist or never happened.

Here's an example. Imagine that you are having a tarot reading, and the reader says:

> "There are indications here of a new professional role. Does this mean something to you?"

For the sake of this example, let us assume that this is incorrect and means nothing to you at all. Here is how the baiting works.

Step 1. Agree enthusiastically and add one more piece of false information. For example, if you happen to be a single woman, you could say:

"That's quite amazing actually, because two weeks ago I got a new job at the same company where my husband works. We were both really pleased."

Step 2. Encourage development of the theme:

"I was hoping you might pick up on that because it has been on my mind a lot. This new job is going to be quite a difficult challenge for me."

With any luck, the psychic will feel encouraged to offer a follow-up line. This may well include the supplementary piece of disinformation you have planted, like this:

"Well, one thing I can see is that both you and your husband are in for a difficult time of transition, but it will be well worth it in the end. The key is to see the challenges as opportunities, which is what they are."

Step 3. Agree, encourage more development, and refer to the alleged mode of the psychic divination. For tarot cards, the reader is supposed to be divining information by looking at the cards. So you say something like:

"I can see that makes a lot of sense. What else can you see in the cards about this new job?"

The psychic now thinks she has hit a home run, so she will be happy to progress:

"I see some minor problems with one of your new colleagues, or with your new boss, but these will be ironed out smoothly in time. Also, while your new role will be satisfying financially, I can tell you that you will also encounter new areas of expenditure. You must learn to take the long-term view."

Step 4. Praise the accuracy of the psychic method in use, be it tarot cards, astrology or whatever. Encourage the psychic to chime in with self-satisfied words confirming the dependability of her psychic modus operandi:

"It's really amazing. I honestly had no idea the tarot could really be so accurate."

"Well, it's never easy to be clear or certain, but the cards are often a wonderful window on to truth."

Step 5. Bide your time, and be content to let the psychic tell you more about your non-existent husband and the non-existent new job. When you judge the time is right, you can confess your surprise:

"Well, I'm confess I am rather puzzled about one thing. I don't have a husband, and I haven't started a new job. How can you see things about a husband and a job that I just made up?"

At this stage, the psychic may realise there's no point in continuing. Alternatively, she may remonstrate and point out that you had previously agreed with her statements. You can say:

"That's right. I just went along with whatever you said. But that doesn't explain how you 'saw' my husband in the cards when I don't even have a husband."

Baiting can only work once the psychic has mentioned something *factual*. It cannot be applied to statements that are hypothetical or that concern the future. You must wait until something is stated as a fact that you know not to be true.

Here's a completely different example. Suppose a highly gifted medium offers you a vague description of someone she says is 'coming through':

"I'm sensing a presence of someone who passed about two years ago, and possibly the problem was in the heart or chest area. It's an elderly gentleman, who at one time had a beard. Does the name Harry or Henry mean something to you?"

Let's assume this name means nothing to you at all.

Step 1. Express agreement, and plant disinformation:

"My goodness! It must be my grandfather, Henry. He passed over just before his wife, Emily."

Step 2. Encourage development:

"The strange thing is that on my way here I had a funny feeling he'd come through."

"Well, he's here now and he wants me to tell you how proud he is of you, but he's concerned that you're working too hard."

Step 3. Agree, and refer to the psychic method in use:

"That's exactly the sort of thing he would say! It's amazing you can get messages through from the other side so clearly."

"Well, don't thank me, I'm just a channel."

Step 4. Praise the accuracy:

"But it's so amazing. I mean, it's almost as if he's here in the room with me."

Step 5. Allow the psychic to add any more details she wishes. When you feel the time is right, say:

"There is one thing that puzzles me a little. I've never had a grandfather called Henry, nor anyone in the family called Emily. So how can you be getting messages from people I have just made up off the top of my head?"

The same basic formula can be applied to any reading. You just have to adjust the details a little, depending on what kind of psychic brilliance is on offer.

What is more, if you do this successfully it will usually cost you nothing. In most cases, the psychic will suddenly develop a marked disinclination to continue, refund your money and bid you farewell.

Progress Review

In Section Four we have looked at ways of stopping cold reading from being used on you. Sections One to Four taken together provide a detailed description of how cold reading works in the psychic industry. There remain a few miscellaneous points to cover, more for the sake of completeness than anything else. These are the subject of Section Five.

Section 5: Additional Notes

"The ability to discriminate between that which is true and that which is false is one of the last attainments of the human mind."

- James Fennimore Cooper, 'The American Democrat'

Additional Notes

The sections you have read so far provide a complete description of how cold reading works and how to prevent it being used on you. In this section, I want to address a few other points that often arise in discussions about cold reading.

They are all points that I should have found a suitable place for elsewhere in this book, and I'm confident that a better writer would have done so. Alas, we must live within our limitations.

Instant readings

The cold reading methods I have described in this book are quite elaborate. They can furnish detailed readings of almost any duration, with 20–30 minutes being typical. However, some psychics specialise in rapid-fire 'instant' readings, such as quick readings given during radio broadcasts.

In these situations, some psychics like to play safe and rely on Barnum Statements, Pollyanna Pearls, Veiled Questions and other elements that lend themselves to instant readings. It is not a problem if the reading comes across as rather bland. The psychic can always claim that she would *normally* provide more detail, but for a lively radio show she has to keep things moving. This may be followed by offers of a personal consultation that I expect will be very reasonably priced.

Others psychics in this situation may throw caution to the winds and include Good Chance Guesses, Lucky Guesses and Folk Stat Statements, taking the risk of being wrong as often as they are right. There is no harm done, since only the impressive hits will be remembered. The psychic can also attribute the misses to the challenge of trying to give quick readings over the airwaves. After all, maybe radio waves sometimes interfere with psychic ones. Who can say for sure?

Stock readings

Psychologist Bertram Forer once gave some students what he said were individual personality profiles specially prepared for each student by an expert. He asked each student to rate the accuracy of his or her own personality profile. The majority of the students were impressed at how well their profile captured the essence of their personality. Forer then revealed that in fact all the students had been given the exact, same personality profile!

If you look up the details of 'The Forer Effect' online, you can read the 'personality profile' that was used in this famous experiment. You may even think that it matches *your* personality quite well!

The personality profile that Forer used was a simple example of a 'stock' reading, meaning a fixed script that is delivered to every client. Reciting the same text to every client is rather boring for the psychic and, if clients should get to compare notes, rather unconvincing. However, stock readings can be used in a more sophisticated way.

Consider a very simplified example. The psychic learns 12 different short readings pertaining to romance, and associates each one with a month of the year. During the reading, she ascertains which month the client was born in. She can then deliver the corresponding stock reading about romance that she has prepared for that particular month. If she also has 12 short readings prepared for health, career and other main themes, she can give quite a substantial reading simply by reciting prepared sets of lines.

A stock system such as this can be made as complex and as sophisticated as the psychic wishes. The only real limitation is her willingness to prepare and memorise lots of stock phrases. For example, instead of just 12 short readings for each major theme, she could prepare 26 and associate each one with a letter of the alphabet. As soon as she knows the first letter of the client's name, she delivers the corresponding stock reading.

If the psychic is using tarot cards, she may learn the supposed 'meaning' of all 78 cards so that she is never lost for something to say. Those who prefer to place less strain on their intellect may choose instead to only prepare stock readings for the 22 tarot cards known as the Major Arcana.

I know at least one practitioner of psychic readings who has spent years writing and collecting literally hundreds of stock phrases and refining them into one vast system. Many stock systems have been devised over the years, and some can be purchased from the nice people who supply goods to the psychic industry or to magicians and mind-readers.

Reasons for using stock readings

Some psychics use stock readings because they believe in the divinatory system they use. For example, the psychic may believe that each tarot card has a specific meaning and that she must convey the meaning accurately (blended with her own interpretation) for the reading to be successful.

This is not actually the case. In reality, one can ascribe almost any plausible meaning to any card without affecting the perceived merit of the reading. The facts of the ritual matter very little. What matters is the client's belief and participation in the ritual and his or her readiness to succumb to its supposed authority or efficacy.

There are similarities here with many other procedures and practices that rely on what is referred to as 'ritual magic'. This term applies to any process or treatment where the benefit, if there is any, derives solely from the participant's *belief* that there will be a benefit. There are many such practices, but it's difficult to cite examples without getting drawn into the kind of arguments I consider it best to avoid.

For example, I would suggest that acupuncture works the same way. Whether one places the needles in accordance with formal acupuncture teachings, or more or less at random, makes little difference to the perceived efficacy of acupuncture treatment. All that matters, I would suggest, is whether the patient *believes* that he or she is receiving genuine, authentic treatment. I expect people within the acupuncture industry will assure you I am completely wrong about this. Maybe they are right. Then again, maybe acupuncture (like psychic ability) is as real as you want it to be.

Another reason why some psychics use stock readings is that they either dislike improvisation or feel unable to improvise successfully. Some practitioners simply feel more comfortable knowing they have a lot of lines memorised and hence will never be at a loss for something to say.

Personally, I have never been a fan of memorising stock elements and scripts. I prefer to improvise because I find it much more interesting and enjoyable. I quite like starting a reading without having the faintest clue what I am going to say. Like so many aspects of this or any other craft, it simply comes down to personal style and preference.

Mnemonics

Some psychics facilitate the cold reading process by using simple tried-and-tested memory systems. I myself have tried using a mnemonic system that gave me one or two key words for every card in a tarot pack. These key words had nothing to do with the actual meanings the cards are supposed to have. They just provided me with prompts for something to say, ensuring that I never ran out of material.

Using mnemonics and relying on stock reading elements can lead to some surprising hits. A talented cold reader I know was once giving readings at a home for senior citizens. He was giving a reading to a very elderly lady when a card came up that was associated in his system with a wedding celebration. Though it seemed clearly inappropriate, he decided to stick to his system and mention a wedding. As soon as he did, everyone roared with laughter and amazement. This very elderly lady had recently announced her engagement to one of the men in the same institution!

Mnemonics can also be used in other ways. Some psychics, who are especially devoted to their work, use simple memory techniques to remember details about their clients and the main themes that came out of the reading. Should the psychic meet the same client again, she can pick up where she left off and avoid saying anything that would contradict her previous reading. Of course, there is no need to use sophisticated memory aids to do this. A set of file cards works just as well if not better, and is easier to use

Meet the expert

If you are interested in memory techniques, then I suggest you refer to the several books published by my friend Dominic O'Brien. Dominic has won the World Memory Championship eight times since its inception in 1991. He secured his first entry in the Guinness Book of Records in 1989, when he memorised the correct sequence of *six* decks of cards randomly shuffled together, or 312 cards in total.

However, Dominic is nothing if not determined to prove that his memory training systems really work, and in 1995 he memorised no less than 40 decks shuffled together. In other words, Dominic was able to recall the correct sequence of 2080 cards having seen each card just once.

He can do sprints as well as marathons. Dominic has memorised the order of 1 deck of cards in 38.29 seconds (verified by Guinness) or 27.5 seconds (personal best). I have seen him do this first-hand, at a private dinner party, and it is a wonderful thing to behold.

For many years I used to organise a rather strange birthday party each year at which I persuaded some of my fellow entertainers to participate in an informal 'cabaret'. One year, Dominic came along and invited two guests to compose a 100 digit number entirely at random. Dominic then committed the entire 100 digit number to memory in 2 minutes. If you do not think that sounds very entertaining, you obviously have never seen the remarkable Mr. O'Brien in action. He won the most fervent and enthusiastic applause I think I have ever witnessed.

I could write much more about the amazing Mr. O'Brien. Suffice it to say that if you want to learn anything about memory techniques then your wisest course is to get hold of Dominic's books and study his methods.

Hot reading

Cold reading concerns readings that are given to complete strangers *without any prior information*. 'Hot reading' is trade jargon for covertly obtaining information about the client before the reading. I have looked into this area and it is quite staggering how much you can find out about someone ahead of time without them knowing. Magicians, con artists, detectives and those in the espionage trade have all devised many excellent ways to gain information about a person without them ever knowing.

There is good evidence to suggest that some psychics use assorted forms of hot reading. If the psychic works from an office, or from her own home, she may employ various simple ruses to glean useful information. For example, the visiting client may be welcomed by a charming assistant who kindly takes her coat and handbag or purse. Unknown to the client, the seemingly innocent assistant rifles through these possessions for any useful clues that can be fed to the psychic just before the reading begins. Another time-honoured trick is for the assistant to briefly peer through the windows of the visiting client's car, just in case it contains any clues to her lifestyle and interests.

Hot spiritualism

Some people who have studied the spiritualist movement suggest that psychics sometimes compile notes on regular clients and circulate them among themselves. Not only does this allow psychics to be exquisitely well-prepared for certain clients, it also means they all come up with readings that seem consistent. This boosts their collective credibility in the eyes of the client.

Anyone interested in this area should read a remarkable and thoroughly entertaining book called 'The Psychic Mafia' by M. Lamar Keane, in which the author, a self-confessed fake medium, claims to lift the lid on fakery within the spiritualism industry. However, I cannot vouch for the accuracy of his account.

Some say that spiritualists have assisted the success of their larger public demonstrations using hot reading techniques, especially if the media are going to be present. For example, the psychic may send free tickets to the event to clients whom she has known for years or even decades. During the show, the psychic seems to be delivering astonishingly accurate readings to complete strangers. In reality, the 'complete stranger' may have been visiting the psychic regularly for the past 20 years.

Psychics who give televised demonstrations of their awesome gift often enjoy opportunities to gain information before the cameras roll. Many TV producers see no harm in allowing the psychic (or associates) to mingle ahead of time with those members of the audience to whom she will give a reading on air.

Even if this kind of pre-show contact is not allowed by the TV production team, the psychic may well notice some useful details ahead of time. For example, she might see some of the production notes regarding who is in the audience, or see a photograph of a deceased relative being handed to the production team so it can be 'grabbed' as a still image and displayed on screen during the show.

One of my correspondents, Ben Whiting, tells me that some travelling fortune-tellers, who call from house to house, leave behind coded information about the occupants of each house they call on. This code, apparently called 'patrin', covers such information as how many people live at that address, the number of children, any recent bereavements or impending marriages and so on. Hence any other fortune-teller who understands the code, and who passes along the same way, has a head start.

The realm of the impossible

From the above discussion, it follows that psychics can, and sometimes do, obtain information about clients beforehand. In general, to assert that it would have been 'impossible' for a psychic to know something about a client in advance is to assert a nonsense. It may be hard to imagine how information could have found its way from A to B, but this is scarcely the same as being impossible.

To illustrate this point, let me share a story with you. I assure you from the outset that this is absolutely true.

I once went to present a lecture show in a smart and well-equipped student theatre. Upon my arrival, I was introduced to a pleasant young woman called Becky who ran the theatre, and with whom I discussed my sound and lighting requirements. Becky was moderately interested in what my show was about, and I suppose that she and I chatted together for at least 20 minutes or so.

If I were in the business of claiming genuine psychic powers, my meeting with Becky would have been a perfect opportunity to demonstrate my 'inexplicable' gifts. I would have been able to tell Becky a huge amount of information about her past life, including dozens of highly specific details. Becky would have been astounded, and she would have sworn that I had never previously met her or anyone she knew. The incident would have seemed an impenetrable mystery and would have made a lovely chapter in any books devoted to my astonishing psychic powers.

The fact is that I *had* known Becky quite well, some 16 years previously. She and I had both attended the same university, and had both been in a medium-sized theatre group putting on a show at the Edinburgh Fringe Festival. Becky simply did not remember me, and had no recollection of the few weeks when we had been in Edinburgh together.

How to account for this? Perhaps it is a testament to my weak personality and general dearth of charisma. Then again, my appearance had changed quite a lot from my student days (and so had Becky's, come to that). Also, some people are just not terribly good at remembering people from the distant past.

Whatever the reasons in this particular case, this story illustrates the fact that you can never be *certain* a psychic is operating without prior knowledge — even if the client herself sincerely believes this to be true.

I myself have never used hot reading, nor has it ever seemed necessary. For the record, my TV demonstrations (such as those transcribed in Section Three) have never involved 'hot' reading or any kind of prior information.

Can anyone learn cold reading?

This question crops up quite often. The answer is the same for cold reading as for anything else: anyone can try to learn it but some will have more natural aptitude than others. Cold reading tends to require the gift of the gab, modest acting ability, lack of nerves and a touch of 'stage presence'. Charm and charisma obviously help, but I seem to have done okay despite a conspicuous lack of both.

It is important to note that different practitioners learn cold reading in different ways. Some learn from books, some are taught, some more or less teach themselves as they go along. Some are very analytical and teach themselves cold reading by studying and practising for many years (which is what I did). Others more or less develop the knack without trying.

Perhaps surprisingly, it is possible to become a skilled cold reader without realising it. Anyone who starts to give readings for fun will get at least a few favourable responses just by chance. If she persists, by trial and error she will slowly develop the knack of saying things that people seem to find meaningful in one way or another. All of this can happen entirely inadvertently. Before long, she will be getting so many favourable reactions to her readings that she will feel entitled to credit herself with some sort of authentic psychic ability.

The best account of this process is probably Susan Blackmore's book, 'The Adventures of a Parapsychologist', in which she explains how she started giving readings for fun and slowly came to believe she must possess psychic ability. In time, she was able to see she was in fact cold reading without even trying.

This is why neither I nor anyone else can point to a psychic and say they are *intentionally* deceiving their clients. To do that I would have to be a genuine mind-reader! What I can say is that *if* there is no such thing as genuine psychic ability (which happens to be my opinion), *then* anyone who claims to be psychic is either deceiving themselves or deceiving others.

Progress Review

This is the end of Section Five. We have seen what cold reading is, how it works in the psychic industry and how it can be prevented from working.

If you have followed all the material in these five sections, you can be confident that you know as much about cold reading as almost anyone else — including those who practise it!

Section 6: Applied Cold Reading

"Reality is that which, when you stop believing in it, doesn't go away."

- Philip K. Dick

Introduction to ACR

This book describes how cold reading works in the psychic industry. However, some cold reading techniques can be applied to other contexts that have nothing to do with psychics and fortune-telling. When cold reading is used *outside the context of the psychic industry*, I call it Applied Cold Reading or ACR for short.

In this concluding section, I just want to introduce the concept of ACR and briefly touch on some of the different forms it can take. I don't propose to provide a comprehensive account of how ACR works. This is a large subject in its own right and it would fall outside the scope of this book. However, I felt it would be appropriate to at least touch on the subject.

A brief history

ACR is something I developed over a period of about twenty years. Here's how it came about.

My first job was in creative media and marketing. I worked for a small company that could create just about anything from printed brochures to corporate videos.

The job involved dealing with clients in many different industries. Here's a small sample: pharmaceuticals, heavy engineering, sports and leisure, footwear, herbicides, adhesives, magazine publishing, pet food, bathroom and shower fittings, retail fashion, dietary supplements, radiators, catering, security printing, milk marketing and glamour photography! As you may have gathered, no two days were ever the same.

Although selling wasn't my full-time job, it was the sort of company where everyone did a bit of everything so I did occasionally try pitching our services to local companies.

At that time in my life, I had already been studying magic for about 15 years. I specialised in the kind of magic that is known in the trade as 'mentalism', which means magic pertaining to psychology and the workings of the mind. I had reached the stage where I was moderately good at mind-reading and things like that. I had also learned how to replicate every psychic ability under the sun, including the art of giving 'spookily accurate' psychic readings.

The more direct selling I did, the more I began to wonder if I could apply some cold reading techniques to the sales process (as well as to other work-related situations). I tentatively began to experiment with this idea. I found that a little cold reading here and there could often help my sales visits to go well. It was good for building rapport and creating a sense of agreement that was highly conducive to getting a deal.

The years went by and my career lurched from one phase to another, as careers tend to do. I fell into the Information Technology (IT) industry where, once again, I was dealing with clients in many different industries. In time I ascended through the levels of my incompetence all the way from humble worker drone to senior management. For a brief period I was even the UK Head of Sales & Marketing for a global internet technologies company.

Throughout this time I was slowly refining my ideas about how to apply cold reading to different aspects of my working life, and not just with regard to selling. I also applied it to some of the situations and challenges that come with a management role.

When I tired of office life, fearing my desiccated soul would never know joy again, I waved goodbye, quit my job and started to work for myself. This entailed having to sell and market my own services (at least in those months when I wanted to eat). I used a lot of what might be called 'conventional' selling and marketing techniques, but again I found a few cold reading touches, judiciously applied, could often help whenever I was trying to sell, persuade or negotiate.

That, in a nutshell, is how I came to develop Applied Cold Reading.

In 2008, at the request of several interested friends, I put together a 2-day training course all about ACR and how to use it. I gave it the rather grand name of the ACR Masterclass.

From my point of view, the great thing about the Masterclass is that it brings me into contact with lots of wonderful people from many different walks of life. The 'students' have included professional sales people, therapists, entertainers, doctors, managers, teachers, entrepreneurs, events organisers, broadcasters… the list could go on and on. At one class I even had a professional poker player! With *very* few exceptions, all these people have told me they find ACR useful and beneficial as well as fun to learn.

Defining ACR

The working definition for ACR is the same as the working definition for 'normal' cold reading, with a little extra addition: 'ACR is the process that occurs within an ACR model. It is a set of strategies, to do with the psychology of communication, that enable you to influence what others think, feel and believe'.

The only part of this definition that is new, assuming you have read the earlier sections of this book, is the term 'ACR model'. So let's see what that means.

The ACR model

There are six basic sections to the ACR Masterclass:

- the ACR model (a way to analyse any specific dialogue or conversation)
- ACR refinements (things that help *any* dialogue to go well)
- AQ (answering questions successfully, in any situation)
- ACR Failsafes (themes and statements that always foster agreement)
- Persuasion Tips (the best simple guidelines I know for being persuasive)
- Rapport Tips (the best simple guidelines I know for building rapport)

The first of these, the ACR model, is the most important and the one that takes up the most time. An ACR model consists of eight separate elements that can be defined for any given conversation or dialgoue. I won't describe the eight elements in detail here, simply because it would take too long (bear in mind that the ACR Masterclass usually lasts for two full working days).

The eight elements of the ACR model allow you to analyse *and prepare for* any given dialogue that crops up in your professional working life. If you do a lot of selling, you can build an ACR model relevant to the typical conversations you have with your customers (or potential customers). If you do a lot of teaching and want to quickly build good rapport with your students, you can build a model to help you achieve this. The same goes for any other trade or profession and the situations you encounter on a regular basis.

You *can* also create ACR models for conversations that crop up in your social life, but the ACR Masterclass usually focuses on the professional domain.

One aim of the Masterclass is that everyone learns how to build their own ACR model suitable for their own professional life and requirements.

Building your first ACR model tends to be a slow process that involves a lot of pencil and paper time plus some head-scratching. Eventually, with practise and experience, the appropriate ACR model for any situation tends to come to mind almost instantly. It's a bit like learning to drive: on your first lesson it can take you half an hour just to get down the street, but with experience you can drive long distances with scarcely any conscious effort.

The purpose of ACR

Expressed in very general terms, the purpose of ACR is to create a positive experience for the person you are talking to.

We all know what negative experiences sound like:

- This guy just doesn't understand me at all

- This guy obviously isn't going to be able to help at all

- This guy plainly hasn't a clue about this company or the situation we're in

- This conversation is just a waste of time

I could provide more examples but I think you get the general idea. Conversely, this is what most positive experiences tend to sound like:

- Great! It so nice to talk to someone who actually understands the situation!

- At last! Someone who can actually help with this problem!

- Wow, she seems to know all about our market. It's nice to meet someone so well-informed!

- He's got some really good ideas that we should really look into!

- We're obviously on the same wavelength. I expect we'll be able to come to a very good agreement.

See the difference? In ACR, when we talk about 'positive experiences' we are referring to feelings of understanding, empathy, being well-informed and being able to help. ACR provides you with tools to help you create these experiences for the people you deal with.

The most important of these tools is the ACR statement. This is a statement that can never be wrong (or, more precisely, never *completely* wrong) and will always allow the conversation to flow forwards in a positive direction. This, in turn, creates a sense of agreement. Agreement is always a positive thing if you are trying to sell, persuade, negotiate or build good rapport. (One good definition of rapport is, 'A mood of agreement sustained over time'.)

ACR is not something you use all the time during a conversation. When I was selling my company's services, I could talk with a potential customer for an hour and perhaps only use ACR once or twice in that time. However, those one or two uses of ACR could often make all the difference between success and failure.

ACR in practice

To see how ACR works in practice, let's start by briefly returning to the psychic context but look at it in a different light.

I said that ACR is about fostering a positive experience. When a client goes for a psychic reading, what sort of positive experience is she looking for? It can vary, but generally she wants some sort of psychic insight that will provide reassurance, comfort or guidance. If she has a specific problem that she isn't sure how to handle, she wants to feel that the psychic will understand her, sympathise, and be able to offer a little bit of advice and hope.

As we have seen, the psychic can provide this positive experience by using the techniques explained in this book. A large part of the process involves making statements that can never be wrong (or at least not *totally* wrong). This creates agreement, which leads to good rapport, which leads to a sense of the reading being productive and useful.

Consider a simple example. The psychic gets into the reading, looks at the client and says:

> "There are indications here of a relationship issue that's on your mind. Can you relate to this?"

Let's pause to consider the possibilities.

Suppose the statement is correct, and the client *does* have a relationship issue on her mind. How will she feel about this statement? She will feel that the psychic really *understands* her, and can *empathise* with her situation.

Since the psychic was somehow able to 'sense' this straight away, the client will also be suitably impressed and more inclined than ever to believe the psychic has an amazing gift. This in turn supports the idea that the psychic is well-qualified to offer help, guidance and reassurance. The client will think to herself, 'At last! I've found the help I've been looking for!'

The psychic has been able to create a mood of understanding, empathy, being well-informed and being able to help. What's more, she has been able to achieve this in *less than five seconds*.

However, suppose the statement is incorrect. The client might say something like:

> *"No, not really, there's nothing like that on my mind at the moment."*

This is not a problem because the psychic can use a revision. She can say:

> "Okay, that's absolutely fine, I agree there may not be anything like that on *your* mind, at least not at the moment. However, relationships obviously do matter to you, and you are the sort of helpful person that other people sometimes turn to for help."

> *"Well, yes, from time to time."*

> "That's really what I was getting at. Someone near you has a relationship matter that they would like to chat to you about. It could come up quite soon. Will you look out for that?"

The psychic has used the Applicability and Time revisions, and managed to insert a little bit of Fine Flattery as well. There is no sense of conflict, argument or disagreement, and the conversation (the reading) can move smoothly forwards, still sounding positive and helpful.

When we use ACR, we essentially use the same general principles to achieve the same result: a positive emotional experience based on feelings of understanding, empathy, rapport, being well-informed and being able to help. What's more, we are able to achieve this result incredibly quickly.

Let's see how this works in a few different contexts.

Direct sales

There are some perfectly straightforward ways to handle any sales situation. You can be polite, pleasant and likeable, ask good questions, listen to the customer and build a picture of what she wants. You can then aim to position your product or service as the remedy to her problem. This is all perfectly good selling philosophy.

ACR does not *replace* this option. It simply gives you an *additional* option. More specifically, it enables you to make ACR statements — ones that can build rapport and a sense of agreement more rapidly than any other technique in the world, and that can never actually be wrong.

A simple example

When I teach ACR, I tend not to feature too many examples for one good reason: what's important to each student is *their* own ACR model that *they* build, and that has relevance to *their* working life. This is far more important and interesting than any number of examples taken from other ACR models and other contexts that may mean nothing to them.

However, for the sake of completeness, I'll offer one very basic and simplified example.

One person who attended the ACR Masterclass ran a kind of residential fitness centre where men and women could go to lose weight and get fit. Let's call her Jane (not her real name). Most of Jane's clients were women, and they usually called her for a chat about the fitness centre and how it worked before they actually committed to booking a place.

In the Masterclass, Jane built her own ACR model for these situations (with a little help from myself and from other students). Jane came up with several good ACR statements. One of them went like this:

> "You've been thinking about this decision for quite a while, haven't you? Discussing it with friends, feeling a bit unsure whether it's right for you. I expect one of your close friends has sort of 'nagged' you into calling me."

Let's pause to consider the possibilities.

Suppose the statement is correct. The caller might well be amazed at Jane's level of insight. She will feel that Jane really understands her, and can empathise precisely with her situation.

This in turn promotes the feeling that she is talking to the right person, and that Jane can really help her. She might well say something like:

"That's true, actually! My friend heard about you and she's been telling me to give you a call."

What has happened here? Jane has managed to create a mood of understanding, empathy, being well-informed and being able to help. What's more, she has been able to do this in about ten seconds.

However, suppose the statement is incorrect? The potential customer might say something like this:

"No, not really. It's not the sort of thing I tend to discuss with people. I just don't know if I can really afford it."

This is not a problem because Jane can use a revision. It might sound like this:

"That's even better. What I meant was that many people who come to see me *do* discuss it with friends first, and in fact many of them only come and see me because their friends kind of push them into it! The fact that you have taken the initiative yourself, *without* any prodding from anyone else, is a really good sign. It's people like you who are probably going to get the most out of what we offer here."

By saying this, the conversation can flow smoothly forward in a positive spirit of agreement. (As you have probably worked out for yourself, in this example Jane used the Applicability revision plus a little bit of Fine Flattery.)

As I said, this is a simplified example. Jane's actual ACR model and the statements in it were a little more complicated, and involved her own detailed knowledge of her market.

Nonetheless, it suffices to illustrate the basic principle. When the statement is correct, it helps to create a tone of understanding, empathy, being well-informed and being able to help. These are all very positive feelings that could greatly assist the selling process. What's more, this only takes a few seconds. When the statement is incorrect, no harm is done and the dialogue can still flow forwards in a positive direction without any lingering sense of conflict or disagreement.

Business to business sales

As I have mentioned before, a lot of my own selling experience was in the area of 'business to business' selling. When I was selling internet technology services, I was sometimes able to go into a sales meeting well-prepared and fully briefed. However, there were times when this simply wasn't possible.

In these situations, where I was not as prepared as I would have preferred, I could of course simply be pleasant (or at least as pleasant as I ever get), ask questions and be a good listener. However, I also had the option of using an ACR statement like this:

> "As I understand it, you [meaning 'your company'] have enjoyed quite a bit of expansion recently."

Let's pause to consider the possibilities.

Suppose the statement is correct. I have created a sense that I know a little bit about the company and its recent successes. In other words, a mood of understanding, empathy, being well-informed and being able to help. These are all positive feelings, so I've put myself in a good position to sell and negotiate.

However, suppose the statement is incorrect. Perhaps the company has in fact experienced some difficulties and has even had to scale down some departments? The client might say:

> "Well, not really. I don't know where you've got that from, we've actually had to cut back a bit."

This is not a problem because I can use a revision:

> "Yes, I agree, you have had to cut back in *operational* terms, I understand that. I was referring to your expansion in terms of the market — you've still got good market share, your brand is still strong and is gaining profile, you are looking to expand your range as soon as you can. There's still a philosophy of expansion and seeing what opportunities there are in the market. That's what I was talking about."

This example uses the Interpretation revision to convert the incorrect statement into one that is correct, or at least sufficiently correct to allow the conversation to flow smoothly forwards.

Incidentally, if you have any experience of selling and textbook sales techniques, you may be familiar with the concept of a 'yes set'. In simple terms this means presenting the customer with a series of propositions you know he will agree with, hoping that he is then 'conditioned' to say yes to the sales proposition at the end of the sequence. ACR sometimes works in a similar way, although in practice it can perhaps be a little more subtle than most 'yes sets' tend to be.

Management

Anyone in management knows that good communication skills are more or less essential. When I was first entrusted with some management responsibilities, I was struck by the variety of working relationships that came with the territory. Sometimes I was talking to subordinates, and had to try and motivate them, oversee them or get them to adopt new policies and procedures. Sometimes I was talking to other managers, some of whom I got along with better than others. Sometimes I was talking to my superiors, those venerated souls higher up the company organisation chart than I was. In addition I had to talk to suppliers, prospects, clients, contacts, ancillary companies and so on.

In many cases, I didn't just need to communicate *well* but also *persuasively*. In this respect, I often found small touches of ACR could be very advantageous. By making a statement or two that created a tone of agreement and empathy, I found it a lot easier to bring negotiations to a happier conclusion.

In recent years, I've had the chance to discuss all sorts of management issues with managers from a wide range of companies, both during the ACR class and in other situations. Many have shared with me examples of how ACR fits in with their personal management style, or how it helped with one situation or another.

Management is, of course, a vast subject in its own right. Recent years have seen something of an explosion in the number of books, courses and management theories that the ambitious manager can spend her time and money studying. Do all these books and theories actually help anyone to be a better manager? It's certainly open to doubt, and if you're interested in this subject I suggest you read 'The Management Myth' by Matthew Stewart. It's the kind of book that may not necessarily have all the right answers, but certainly asks some excellent questions.

Therapy

I have never worked in any therapeutic field, so I have no direct first-hand experience to share. However, many therapists have attended the ACR Masterclass, including hypnotherapists, practitioners of NLP (neuro-linguistic programming), occupational therapists, educational therapists who help people with learning difficulties, counsellors who specialise in various different fields and many more besides. They tell me that ACR helps them in two ways.

First of all, many of these therapists are self-employed and therefore spend part of their time selling their services to potential clients. In many cases the customer's decision simply comes down to whether he or she feels a sense of rapport with the therapist. Hence it is obviously useful if the therapist can create a mood of understanding, empathy, being well-informed and being able to help.

Secondly, in the process of actually providing therapeutic or counselling services, the bond between client and therapist is very important. If the bond is good, the treatment stands a good chance of success. If not, it's highly unlikely anything good will come of it. This is far more important in the therapeutic world than in the relatively impersonal world of selling cars or photocopiers. Hence it very useful if the therapist knows how to build good rapport very quickly, and sustain it. I believe that ACR helps people to do precisely this.

Criminal interrogation

Some time ago, someone suggested that ACR might possibly be used in conjunction with the questioning of suspects during police investigations.

During one of my visits to the United States, I had the privilege of discussing this possibility with Peter Kougasian, Assistant DA for the County of New York. Peter suggested I get hold of a copy of 'Criminal Interrogation and Confessions' by Inbau, Reid and Buckley, which is a standard textbook on the subject (I will abbreviate the authors' names to 'IRB').

When I studied the book, I noticed some interesting parallels between cold reading and the advice given to officers who handle the questioning of suspects. For example, in one section IRB describe the 'Attitude and General Conduct of the Interrogator'. They mention points such as keeping the mood calm but focused, minimising distractions and not doing anything that could either convey anxiety or promote it (for example the interrogator should avoid pacing round the room).

The authors also say the interrogator should use the kind of language and vocabulary that the suspect would use. There are many parallels here with the sections in this book regarding The Set Up and Presentation (for example 'Setting the client at ease', 'Keeping it clear' and 'Keeping it folksy').

ACR, as I have already shown, is about establishing a mood of understanding, empathy, being well-informed and being able to help. At first glance, this might not seem very relevant to the questioning of suspects. However, one thing the book makes clear is that in many investigations it is important for the officer to create rapport with the person he is questioning. Bear in mind that in many cases the person being questioned is *not* the main figure the police want to convict. Getting information from him may be more important than securing a conviction.

In this context, a good ACR statement might run along these lines:

> "Look, I can understand how someone like you — basically a decent, regular guy — can get into these situations. It happens all the time. At first it's just a few short-cuts here and there, a few ways to make a buck. So you bend a few rules now and again, so what? Everyone does it, right? Then you get dragged in a little deeper. One thing leads to another, things get out of hand. People keep telling you everything's going to work out okay, but a few things start to go wrong and now you're here, facing a choice. You can carry on, running and hiding, worrying in case you make one small slip. Or, you can sort this thing out now, draw a line and put it behind you."

This owes a lot to the Jaques Statement that we saw back in the section on 'Statements about character'. In many cases, so my sources tell me, a statement like this is going to be quite an accurate account of what happened. Of course, the suspect might not respond and might maintain an antagonistic stance. However, there's a chance this will create a tone of agreement that makes him just a little bit more likely to co-operate.

You may be interested, as I was, in the legality of using such techniques in the course of a criminal interrogation. IRB deal with this point in admirable detail. Obviously I cannot reproduce all of the relevant legal arguments here. In essence, it seems that interrogators *can* legally employ ruses like this within certain limits. As the authors explain:

"The Supreme Court of the United States in 'Frazier .v. Cupp' recognised the essentiality of interrogation practices involving trickery or deceit, and approved of them" / "the deceit must not be of such a nature as to 'shock the conscience' of the court or the community, nor can it be one that is apt to induce a false confession."

I have not found out if there is any more recent ruling that over-rides this one.

Criminal profiling

Malcolm Gladwell is a best-selling author whose fascinating books, such as 'The Tipping Point' and 'Outliers', have won widespread critical and public acclaim. In the Nov 12th, 1997 edition of 'The New Yorker', he published a remarkable article entitled, 'Dangerous Minds: Criminal Profiling Made Easy'.

In one part of this article, Gladwell suggested that the 'science' of criminal profiling might have much in common with cold reading. I corresponded with Gladwell while he was preparing this article, and in the article itself he was kind enough to mention this book. The article was subsequently reprinted in 'What The Dog Saw', a 2009 compilation of some of Gladwell's 'New Yorker' pieces.

In his article, Gladwell mentions an interesting experiment conducted by Laurence Alison, a University of Liverpool psychologist. He presented a group of senior police officers with details of a crime, the criminal profile drawn up by the FBI, and a description of the offender. Alison asked the officer to rate the accuracy of the criminal profile. The consensus was that the profile was highly accurate. Alison repeated the experiment with a second group of officers. This time he presented exactly the same details of the crime and the criminal profile, but with a completely fictitious description of the offender. This description bore no resemblance to the real criminal. Once again the officers were asked to rate the accuracy of the profile, and once again they concluded that it was highly accurate.

I recommend that you buy 'What The Dog Saw' and read the article for yourself. Like the other articles in the book, it is fascinating, insightful and provocative.

I cannot say whether or not criminal profiling is a legitimate science or whether is assists the apprehension of bad people. For what it's worth, I find myself sympathetic to Gladwell's suggestion that there are some intriguing parallels between the reports produced by the profilers and some of the techniques and terminology used by cold readers.

The PUA community

In case you are unaware, as I was until about five years ago, 'PUA' stands for 'Pick-up Artist'. The PUA community essentially revolves around fascination with the best and most effective ways to approach women in social situations and engineer a successful outcome (howsoever this may be defined).

Ever since I published the first edition of this book, I've been told that it is referred to now and again within the PUA community. Apparently, some leading lights of the PUA community have been kind enough to recommended this book to their many followers. I am very grateful to them.

My lack of involvement with the PUA movement does not arise from a sense of disapproval. I know some people despise the PUA movement on ethical grounds, claiming that it is the very epitome of sleaze. My understanding is that while the PUA community may include some drooling Neanderthals, it also includes many decent and caring men who just happen to lack confidence in social settings. They are looking for a committed and fulfilling relationship, and are interested in PUA wisdom only to the extent that it may help them look relaxed and confident rather than anxious and tongue-tied.

In short, one cannot dismiss the entire PUA community as 'sleazy'. There may be sleazy individuals, but you could probably say the same about any given group of bus drivers, librarians or trombone players.

Can ACR contribute to successful PUA activity? I can't speak from experience, but many PUA experts tell me that yes, most certainly, a little ACR here and there can be very helpful indeed. This does not surprise me, since I maintain you can build an ACR model for just about any kind of inter-personal dialogue.

A happy coincidence

My interest in, and awareness of, the PUA community was boosted by a happy coincidence. In 2010, I flew to the US to lecture to FBI agents on persuasion techniques and some aspects of ACR. This was part of a week of FBI training events involving a wide range of lecturers, one of whom was Neil Strauss. As well as being a very successful journalist, Neil is the author of 'The Game', the best-selling book that first brought the PUA movement to widespread public attention. I was lucky enough to spend a little time with Neil and it was a pleasure to meet him.

When I read 'The Game', I thought it was a hugely impressive achievement. It has great scope and depth and is written with great insight into how people tick. I recommend the book whether or not you have any specific interest in the PUA community. If nothing else, you will gain many insights into what one might call 'real world' human psychology.

One thing I learned from 'The Game' is that many PUAs are interested in learning simple magic tricks they can use when they talk to women. This may sound a little unlikely. One might suppose that trying to impress a woman with a card trick is about as promising as painting the words 'Clueless loser' across your forehead in green ink. However, this isn't *quite* true. When you know the *right* kind of magic tricks and how to present them *well*, they can indeed be an excellent and imaginative way to create interest, fun and a touch of intrigue.

Some people have suggested I write something intended mainly for the PUA community. Perhaps it could include one section on ACR techniques applicable to the PUA context and another section on 'mind-reading' ruses that I know people like. I haven't done this yet, but maybe one of these days I will.

Learning ACR

If you are interested in learning ACR, I invite you to visit the official ACR website: www.appliedcoldreading.com. It will tell you all you need to know. Alternatively, contact me directly (an email would be a good way to start) and we can discuss options. I'm happy to arrange classes for individuals or corporate groups.

Pass It On

Do you like this book? If you do, I want to ask you to help me tell other people about it.

Since 1998, I've sold this book to customers in over 60 countries around the world. However, I have never advertised it anywhere. Every sale has come from 'word of mouth' recommendation. So now I'm asking **YOU** to please help me spread the word!

I bet you have an email list of friends and contacts. Why not send round a 'group email' about this book and its contents?

Post messages about it on web forums and message boards!

Mark your copy so people know it's your property, and leave it in any 'common' area where you work, play or meet other people. It could be quite a conversation starter!

Got friends or contacts in the media? Tell them about this book. They might get a good story, article or feature out of it! (If anyone wants an interview I am easily contacted via my website.)

Do you contribute to a magazine? Why not write a short review of the book, and mention how to order a copy?

Ever call phone-ins and shows about psychics? See if you can squeeze in a mention of this book! Remember, if people just know how to spell 'Rowland', they can easily find my website.

Are you a student or teacher? Maybe this book could be a 'set text' for a course module, or provide the basis for some interesting research and practical social experiments!

THANK YOU!

Ian Rowland

www.thecoldreadingconnection.com

www.ianrowland.com

Curtain Down

This brings to a close the sixth edition of the Full Facts Book of Cold Reading. I hope that you found it interesting and worthwhile.

If you want to get in touch, please visit my website (www.ianrowland.com) and use the email link.

May I once again thank all of those who helped to produce this book, and most of all I would like to thank you for reading it.

Ian Rowland

June 2015, London

Appendix

Note 1: Market for psychic readings

The estimate of '1.4 to 2 billion dollars' was cited in 'The Skeptical Inquirer' Vol. 22, No.3 May/June 1998. Published by the Committee for the Scientific Investigation of Claims of the Paranormal (CSICOP), Buffalo, New York.

Note 2: Deception and entertainment

In 'What this book is not about: Magicians and their methods' I made a distinction between deception used purely for entertainment purposes and deception used outside the sphere of entertainment. It is only fair to note that not every practitioner of the deceptive arts recognises this distinction, or would draw the same boundaries. Among the community of performers given to simulating 'psychic' demonstrations, there are many shades of opinion about the ethics of claims and disclaimers.

Some feel obliged to offer emphatic denials of any 'real' psychic ability. Others encourage the belief that they possess authentic psychic gifts. Many choose a middle-ground policy of 'nothing stated, nothing denied'.

All one can really say is that each performer makes his own choice, and each choice has its consequences. Personally, I do think it's risky to take the 'this is for real' route, since it tends to attract some very strange people and weird requests.

Note 3: Making people like you

In the section on 'Meeting and greeting' I referred to Nicholas Boothman's book, 'How to Make Anyone Like You in 90 Seconds Or Less'. The cover blurb says, 'Learn to read body language, synchronize behaviour and make warm, meaningful connections. For all occasions, business, social and personal'. I have reservations about some of the material, but I think it's a fine introduction to non-verbal communication and techniques for promoting good rapport.

Note 4: Sheehy's 'Passages'

Under 'Jacques Statements' I referred to Gail Sheehy's book 'Passages', which I recommend highly. Sheehy has in fact published several titles in similar vein. 'New Passages' is advertised as a sequel reflecting the social and cultural shifts since the original was published, and I think it's just as valuable. She has also published 'Passages for Men', but I have not read this.

Note 5: Barnum experiments

In the section devoted to 'Barnum statements' I mentioned that psychologists have studied the Barnum Effect. Summaries of at least two such studies appear in Ray Hyman's article, 'Cold Reading: How to Convince Strangers that You Know All About Them' which was published in The Zetetic, Spring–Summer 1977. Among other studies, Hyman refers to:

- Forer, B.R. 1949. 'The Fallacy of Personal Validation: A Classroom Demonstration of Gullibility.' Journal of Abnormal and Social Psychology 44: 118-23.

- Snyder, C.R. and R.J. Shenkel 1975, 'The Barnum Effect', Psychology Today 8: 52:54.

'The Zetetic' was the original name of the journal which changed its name to 'The Skeptical Inquirer'.

In the previous editions of this book, I wrote that I did not know the origin of the term 'Barnum Statement'. Julien Nino got in touch to provide what may well be the answer. He sent me an extract from 'The American Psychologist', Vol 11., No.6, June 1956. In an article entitled 'Wanted - A Good Cookbook', Paul E. Meehl writes, "Many psychometric reports bear a disconcerting resemblance to what my colleague Donald G. Paterson calls 'personality description after the manner of P.T. Barnum'. I suggest - and I am quite serious - that we adopt the phrase 'Barnum effect' to stigmatize those pseudo-successful clinical procedures in which personality descriptions from tests are made to fit the patient largely or wholly by virtue of their triviality."

Note 6: 'Sherlock Strategy' Game answers

In the 'Sherlock Strategy' section I described some clues a cold reader might exploit using the 'Sherlock Strategy'. Here are some possible interpretations. Feel free to disagree!

1. Client plays the violin or viola, and has done for some time.

Years of holding the violin against the neck can result in a very distinctive patch of discolouration on the neck. Violinists may also have distinctive groove marks along the pads of their left fingertips caused by the violin strings. Note that whether a violinist is naturally left- or right-handed, they all play the same way (violin in left hand, bow in right).

2. Client has been buying cosmetics and testing different shades on the back of her hand.

If the marks are on her left hand she is right-handed, and vice-versa. Foundation, concealer, eye-shadow and so on can all be tested in this way.

3. Client has recently visited a dress-maker, to have something made or altered.

In a dress-maker's or outfitter's shop, it is common practice to have the customer take off her shoes and stand on a small raised platform wearing the item to be altered. The dress-maker, while pinning the material to the correct length as required, may use a marking device that puffs a faint horizontal line of chalk on to the material.

4. Client works as a hairdresser, or some other trade that involves handling scissors or shears.

5. It is a relatively safe bet that the client has similar marks on her back.

An experienced cold reader might find it interesting that the birthmark has neither been concealed with cosmetics nor surgically removed. Perhaps the client is a very secure, well-balanced person lacking egotism or vanity. Or she may crave cosmetic surgery but be unable to afford it. It is very likely that someone with this kind of birthmark was instructed from an early age about dermatological care, and so she may be a little more medically aware than most people.

6. It could mean nothing at all - lots of people chew gum just because they like to.

Alternatively, it may indicate one of several possible traits. If she is a considerate smoker, she may use mints or gum to freshen her breath before meetings. The client may also use mints or gum if she is fond of very spicy food, or if she has ever been told (or suspects) she has a bad breath problem.

7. Client has been chalking the tip of a cue, as used to play pool, billiards or snooker.

This is hardly a sure-fire indication, and not a very likely one either. Not many people would schedule a psychic reading after a game of pool! Nonetheless, it may be worth bearing in mind, especially since pool is (at the time of writing) one of the fastest-growing recreations and one enjoyed by both men and women.

8. This clue gives rise to at least two interesting possibilities.

One is that the client reads a newspaper that, being printed using older types of web offset printing and inks, leaves ink smudges on the hands as it is being read. The paper can also leave marks on outer clothing as it is being carried or placed in one's coat pocket. In England, where I live, some daily papers are sufficiently 'wet' to make this quite a serious nuisance. Other daily papers use better printing, or better inks, and never give rise to this problem. This difference makes it possible to guess which newspaper the client reads. In class-ridden and class-obsessed England, this can provide clues as to the client's educational level, political leanings and inclination to peer at photos of semi-naked women over breakfast.

Another possibility is that the client works with the kinds of office printers or copiers that require toner cartridges to be changed once in a while. As many readers will know, toner is a magical substance with properties baffling to conventional science. Though in theory encased within a sealed plastic replacement unit, toner can find its way on to any clean surface or clothing within a five foot radius. It is also well-documented that toner may refuse to attach itself to paper (hence 57 attempts to print a simple letter) but will smear itself into a clean shirt or suit with startling rapidity.

This concludes the 'Sherlock Strategy' Guessing Game. You may think that some or all of these examples are silly and impractical. I would tend to agree, which is why I made it clear the quiz was only presented as a bit of fun. These kinds of clues can be fun to make up or quiz your friends about, but their practical application to skilled cold reading is perhaps more limited than some sources suggest.

Thanks and Acknowledgements

I wish to offer sincere thanks to the following people, all of whom contributed to this book whether they realise it or not.

My first thanks go to my partner in life and in love, Careena, who means everything to me. Together forever, 'g & s'.

James Randi wrote several books that changed my life, and has been a valued friend and source of inspiration for many years. Martin Gardner wrote the 'Mathematical Games' columns that opened the doors to many lasting treasures and was another major influence. Uri Geller changed my life and in recent years has also proved to be a good friend. David Berglas remains the greatest magical performer I have ever seen, and has been a friend and advisor for countless years. Mike Oldfield, a magician who works with music, was another major influence on my aspirations, dreams and magical thoughts.

Lewis Jones taught me more about sneaky deceptive stuff than anyone else.

Penn and Teller I would like to thank chiefly just for being Penn and Teller, thereby teaching what can only be taught by doing it. Nihil me paenitet sane tanta, qua mihi faciebas.

David Britland was a great source of early advice and inspiration. Derek Lever did much to encourage my early interest in magic and has always offered help and support. Derren Brown shared wisdom and fun on many occasions.

Anthony Owen and Marc Paul live, breathe and sleep magic, and are often kind enough to share their expertise with me. Duncan Trillo has provided lots of help over the years and is also to be congratulated on running 'Magic Week' so successfully.

Chris French and Richard Wiseman, both highly-respected authorities in parapsychology, have given freely of their time and expertise over the years.

Michael Shermer made my initial visits to LA very happy ones, and also produces 'The Skeptic', one of the best magazines this world has to offer. The late Marcello Truzzi showed great kindness on many occasions and offered constructive criticism.

Eddie Izzard was the first to get me up on a stage doing fun stuff. I am very pleased for his continued success.

Rory Raven is a great friend, superb mentalist and delightful correspondent. Tom Cutts is another valued friend who has shared many adventures and excellent bottles of wine. Thanks also to the amazing Joshua Quinn, a great friend, brilliant magician and amazingly talented pianist.

Drew McAdam is as daft as a brush, but also an extraordinarily supportive friend.

Massimo Polidoro and Luigi Garlaschelli have helped me on many occasions, and are both wonderful guys to know with a wickedly Italian sense of fun.

Lynne Kelly has been the finest and dearest of friends for what seems like forever, as well as my most tireless correspondent. My thanks go to her and to all the very helpful members of The Garret Community. Alan Jackson is a wonderful source of deep thoughts and obscure information.

Larry Becker never ceases to inspire me with his warm friendship and highly creative contributions to our art. The late Martin Breese was not only my favourite raconteur but also gave freely of his wisdom and advice on countless occasions.

Peter Kougasian also made me feel very welcome to that great city, and has proved to be a terrific friend and supporter.

Matt Field was a wonderful friend and supporter during his tenure as Editor of The Magic Circular, and kindly invited me to write for the magazine. Stan Allen was also kind enough to invite me to scribble articles for MAGIC magazine.

Jeff McBride has been a very supportive friend for many years, and the amazing Banachek has been an ever-helpful colleague in the mind-reading arts. Max Maven is another very valued colleague whose knowledge of our art is second to none.

I can't list all of my friends in the world of magic, but I wish to thank Greg Wilson, David Williamson, David Stone and Michael Weber for many kinds of inspiration as well as sharing many wonderful magical moments. Thanks also to Armando Lucero for being a friend and a peerless magical artist.

I want to thank my friends Jeff and Tessa Evason, the finest mind-readers I know, and Simon Lovell for being my favourite bad influence for many years. Ian Kendall has always been a consistently loyal friend and source of fun, and the same is true of Micke Askernas, the only person I know who can talk as much nonsense as I can.

Thanks also to magical friends Angelo Carbone, Joan du Kore, Ron First, Jorge Garcia, Lennart Green, Jaq Greenspon, Lee

Hathaway, Brad Henderson, Neil Henry, Joshua Jay, Harry Lucas, Lior Manor, Rick Maue, The Mind Artist, Scot Morris, Francisco Nardi, 'Magic Babe' Ning, Shoot Ogawa, Richard Osterlind, Mark Raffles, Per Johan Rasmark, Jamie Raven, Graham Reed, David Regal, Barrie Richardson, Apollo Robbins, Todd Robbins, Romany the Diva of Magic, Marc Salem, Karl Scott, Marc Spelmann, Jim Steinmeyer, Tom Stone, Juan Esteban Varela, Lee Warren and Darius Ziatabari, as well as all my friends at the Magic Circle.

Thanks to 'Myrna Retina' for all the good times shared and unbelievable conversations in well-chosen restaurants. Thanks also to Janet B., Suka, Heather, Janet K., Lupin, Federica and Malin for bringing many kinds of magic into my life.

I wish to thank everyone who has helped me to visit distant lands, offering me their hospitality, assistance and laughter, especially Berk Eratay and all the guys in Turkey, Gay Ljungberg, Markku Purho, Peter Rodgers, Dr. K. Sagathevan, Mario Unger and Roy Zaltsman, plus everyone involved in my trips to Komodo Island and Easter Island. Thanks also to Trinculo, my excellent Travelling Companion Bear, for all his hard work over the years.

Thanks also to those who have invited me to speak, lecture or perform overseas. I may not be able to visit everywhere on the face of the planet before I die, but I'm determined to see as much of it as I possibly can. Invitations to speak or perform in interesting foreign places are therefore always very welcome.

Quotations

The quotations that appear at the front of each section are taken from "Be Reasonable - selected quotations for inquiring minds" edited by Laird Wilcox & John George, © 1994 by Laird Wilcox and John George. Published 1994 by Prometheus Books, New York.

Printed in Great Britain
by Amazon.co.uk, Ltd.,
Marston Gate.